I0415895

February 2012

EMERGENCY COMMUNICATIONS

Various Challenges Likely to Slow Implementation of a Public Safety Broadband Network

GAO
Accountability ★ Integrity ★ Reliability

GAO-12-343

EMERGENCY COMMUNICATIONS

Various Challenges Likely to Slow Implementation of a Public Safety Broadband Network

GAO
Accountability • Integrity • Reliability

Highlights

Highlights of GAO-12-343, a report to congressional requesters

Why GAO Did This Study

Emergency responders across the nation rely on land mobile radio (LMR) systems to gather and share information and coordinate their response efforts during emergencies. These public safety communication systems are fragmented across thousands of federal, state, and local jurisdictions and often lack "interoperability," or the ability to communicate across agencies and jurisdictions. To supplement the LMR systems, in 2007, radio frequency spectrum was dedicated for a nationwide public safety broadband network. Presently, 22 jurisdictions around the nation have obtained permission to build public safety broadband networks on the original spectrum assigned for broadband use. This requested report examines (1) the investments in and capabilities of LMR systems; (2) plans for a public safety broadband network and its expected capabilities and limitations; (3) challenges to building this network; and (4) factors that affect the prices of handheld LMR devices. GAO conducted a literature review, visited jurisdictions building broadband networks, and interviewed federal, industry, and public safety stakeholders, as well as academics and experts.

What GAO Recommends

The Department of Homeland Security (DHS) should work with partners to identify and communicate opportunities for joint procurement of public safety LMR devices. In commenting on a draft of this report, DHS agreed with the recommendation. GAO also received technical comments, which have been incorporated, as appropriate, in the report.

View GAO-12-343 . For more information, contact Mark L. Goldstein at (202) 512-2834 or goldsteinm@gao.gov.

What GAO Found

After the investment of significant resources—including billions of dollars in federal grants and approximately 100 megahertz of radio frequency spectrum—the current land mobile radio (LMR) systems in use by public safety provide reliable "mission critical" voice capabilities. For public safety, mission critical voice communications must meet a high standard for reliability, redundancy, capacity, and flexibility. Although these LMR systems provide some data services, such as text and images, their ability to transmit data is limited by the channels on which they operate. According to the Department of Homeland Security (DHS), interoperability among LMR systems has improved due to its efforts, but full interoperability of LMR systems remains a distant goal.

Multiple federal entities are involved with planning a public safety broadband network and while such a network would likely enhance interoperability and increase data transfer rates, it would not support mission critical voice capabilities for years to come, perhaps even 10 years or more. A broadband network could enable emergency responders to access video and data applications that improve incident response. Yet because the technology standard for the proposed broadband network does not support mission critical voice capabilities, first responders will continue to rely on their current LMR systems for the foreseeable future. Thus, a broadband network would supplement, rather than replace, current public safety communication systems.

There are several challenges to implementing a public safety broadband network, including ensuring the network's interoperability, reliability, and security; obtaining adequate funds to build and maintain it; and creating a governance structure. For example, to avoid a major shortcoming of the LMR systems, it is essential that a public safety broadband network be interoperable across jurisdictions and devices by following five key elements to interoperable networks: governance, standard operating procedures, technology, training, and usage. With respect to creating a governance structure, pending legislation—the Middle Class Tax Relief and Job Creation Act of 2012, among other things—establishes a new entity, the First Responder Network Authority, with responsibility for ensuring the establishment of a nationwide, interoperable public safety broadband network.

The price of handheld LMR devices is high—often thousands of dollars—in part because market competition is limited and manufacturing costs are high. Further, GAO found that public safety agencies cannot exert buying power in relationship to device manufacturers, which may result in the agencies overpaying for LMR devices. In particular, because public safety agencies contract for LMR devices independently from one another, they are not in a strong position to negotiate lower prices and forego the quantity discounts that accompany larger orders. For similar situations, GAO has recommended joint procurement as a cost saving measure because it allows agencies requiring similar products to combine their purchase power and lower their procurement costs. Given that DHS has experience in emergency communications and relationships with public safety agencies, it is well-suited to facilitate joint procurement of handheld LMR devices.

Contents

Tables

Figures

Abbreviations

APCO	Association of Public-Safety Communications Officials
BTOP	Broadband Technology Opportunities Program
CAP	Compliance Assessment Program
COPS	Community Oriented Policing Services
Commerce	Department of Commerce
DHS	Department of Homeland Security
DOT	Department of Transportation
GSA	General Services Administration
ECPC	Emergency Communications Preparedness Center
ERIC	Emergency Response Interoperability Center
FEMA	Federal Emergency Management Agency
FCC	Federal Communications Commission
GHz	gigahertz
HHS	Department of Health and Human Services
kHz	kilohertz
LMR	land mobile radio
LTE	Long Term Evolution
MHz	megahertz
NIST	National Institute of Standards and Technology
NTIA	National Telecommunications and Information Administration
NPSTC	National Public Safety Telecommunications Council
OEC	Office of Emergency Communications
OIC	Office of Interoperability and Compatibility
OJP	Office of Justice Programs
P25	Project 25
PSHSB	Public Safety and Homeland Security Bureau
PSCR	Public Safety Communications Research
PSST	Public Safety Spectrum Trust
USDA	Department of Agriculture
UHF	ultra high frequency
VHF	very high frequency

United States Government Accountability Office
Washington, DC 20548

February 22, 2012

Congressional Requesters

Communication systems are essential for public safety officials—
especially first responders such as police officers and firefighters—to
gather and share information and coordinate their response efforts to
save lives during emergencies. Currently, the public safety community
uses radio frequency spectrum to transmit and receive critical voice
communications through land mobile radio (LMR) systems that are
operated by and licensed to state and local jurisdictions.[1] However, such
LMR systems can have issues with compatibility, continuity, and capacity
in times of large scale emergencies or disasters.[2] In particular, LMR
systems often lack "interoperability"—that is, they lack the capabilities that
allow first responders to communicate with their counterparts in other
agencies and jurisdictions as authorized. Notably, during the terrorist
attacks of September 11, 2001, and Hurricane Katrina in 2005, the lack of
interoperable public safety communications hampered rescue efforts and
the overall effectiveness of public safety operations. Indeed, public safety
communication systems are fragmented across thousands of federal,
state, and local jurisdictions. This fragmentation hampers operations and
puts emergency responders and the public at risk when the responders
cannot talk to one another. More than 7 years after the bipartisan 9/11
Commission reported that compatible and adequate communications
among public safety organizations at the local, state, and federal levels
need to be addressed, the United States still lacks interoperable public
safety communications despite substantial investment by emergency
response agencies to improve their LMR systems.[3] One factor
contributing to continued interoperability issues between jurisdictions is

---

[1]The radio frequency spectrum is the part of the natural spectrum of electromagnetic
radiation lying between the frequency limits of 3 kilohertz (kHz) and 300 gigahertz (GHz).
Radio signals travel through space in the form of waves. These waves vary in length, and
each wavelength is associated with a particular radio frequency.

[2]Capacity refers to a communication system's ability to handle demand, provide coverage,
and send different types of information.

[3]9/11 Commission, *The 9/11 Commission Report: Final Report of the National
Commission on Terrorist Attacks Upon the United States* (Washington, D.C.: July 2004).

the slow progress in developing standards for the communication devices that operate on these LMR systems.

LMR systems currently have the capacity to handle only minimal data transmissions. To supplement the current LMR systems, plans for a second communication system that would provide nationwide broadband services are underway. Such a network would operate on a different portion of the radio frequency spectrum from the LMR systems. In 2007, the Federal Communications Commission (FCC) assigned a portion of spectrum in the upper 700 megahertz (MHz) band exclusively to public safety for broadband use.[4] Some stakeholders advocated for an additional block of spectrum—known as the "D Block"—to be dedicated to public safety. In March 2008, FCC attempted to auction the D Block with public safety encumbrances but failed to attract a winning commercial bidder.[5] Pending legislation, the Middle Class Tax Relief and Job Creation Act of 2012, includes a provision reallocating the D Block to public safety.[6] Public safety officials believe a public safety broadband network would support important data transmission during emergencies, provide first responders with information not currently available (such as vital signs of critically injured people), and foster greater interoperability. However, FCC has estimated that a stand-alone broadband network would cost approximately $15 billion to construct.[7] Furthermore, due to its

---

[4]Congress, in the Balanced Budget Act of 1997, Pub. L. No. 105-33, 111 Stat. 251, mandated that FCC allocate 24 MHz of spectrum for public safety services by January 1, 1998.

[5]See Auction 73, 700 MHz Band, at (last accessed Feb. 17, 2012) http://wireless.fcc.gov/auctions/default.htm?job=auction_summary&id=73.

[6]As of February 17, 2012, the House of Representatives and the Senate had adopted the conference report accompanying the Middle Class Tax Relief and Job Creation Act of 2012, but the legislation had not been signed by the President at the time our work was completed on February 21, 2012. H.R. Rep. 112-399, accompanying the Middle Class Tax Relief and Job Creation Act of 2012, H.R. 3630, 112th Cong. (2012) as reported out on February 16, 2012.

[7]FCC, *A Broadband Network Cost Model: A Basis for Public Funding Essential to Bringing Nationwide Interoperable Communications to America's First Responders*, OBI Technical Paper No. 2 (May 2010). FCC staff told us they believe, based on information in the marketplace, that the cost of the network has risen since the May 2010 publication. The Middle Class Tax Relief and Job Creation Act authorizes $7 billion for the construction of the network from the potential proceeds of "incentive auctions." Incentive auctions are a special type of auction in which an existing user could receive a portion of the proceeds from the auction if the user relinquishes its rights to the spectrum.

technical limitations, the broadband network would not replace the LMR systems for the foreseeable future. A number of jurisdictions sought permission from FCC to begin constructing local or regional public safety broadband networks. and since May 2010, FCC has granted permission to 22 jurisdictions.

Given the important issues surrounding the development of a public safety broadband network, you asked us to provide information about current and planned public safety communication networks and the progress being made to support both voice and data needs. We examined (1) the resources that have been provided for current public safety communication systems and their capabilities and limitations, (2) how a nationwide public safety broadband network is being planned and its anticipated capabilities and limitations, (3) the challenges to building a nationwide public safety broadband network, and (4) the factors that influence competition and cost in the development of public safety communication devices and the options that exist to reduce prices.

To address these objectives, we met with officials and reviewed documentation from 6 of the 22 jurisdictions that received permission from FCC to begin deploying a 700 MHz public safety broadband network, including the San Francisco Bay area, California; Adams County, Colorado; Iowa; Boston, Massachusetts; Mississippi; and Texas. We selected locations based on several criteria, including whether they received federal funding and the size of the planned broadband network. In all of the locations, we interviewed government agencies involved with planning a broadband network, and in locations where planning had progressed, we also interviewed emergency responders who were part of the planning process and vendors selected to build the network, among others. We also interviewed federal agencies involved in public safety communications issues, including entities within the Department of Commerce (Commerce)—the National Institute of Standards and Technology (NIST), the National Telecommunications and Information Administration (NTIA), and the Public Safety Communications Research (PSCR) program; the Departments of Homeland Security (DHS) and Justice; and FCC. In addition, we reviewed relevant documents from these federal entities, including several FCC rulemakings related to developing a broadband network and public safety device competition. We reviewed relevant legislation and conducted a literature review of 43 articles from governmental and academic sources related to emergency communication networks and devices. We interviewed representatives of public safety associations, researchers and consultants recognized for their expertise in public safety communications, and manufacturers of public safety devices, as well as private sector analysts who track this industry. We identified experts and industry stakeholders based on prior published literature, stakeholder recognition and affiliation with the emergency communications and public safety spectrum, and other stakeholders' recommendations. Further details of our scope and methodology are provided in appendix I.

We conducted this performance audit from March 2011 to February 2012 in accordance with generally accepted government auditing standards. Those standards require that we plan and perform the audit to obtain sufficient, appropriate evidence to provide a reasonable basis for our findings and conclusions based on our audit objectives. We believe that the evidence obtained provides a reasonable basis for our findings and conclusions based on our audit objectives.

Background

Currently, public safety officials primarily communicate with one another using LMR systems that support voice communication and usually consist of handheld portable radios, mobile radios, base stations, and repeaters, as described:[8]

- Handheld portable radios are typically carried by emergency responders and tend to have a limited transmission range.

- Mobile radios are often located in vehicles and use the vehicle's power supply and a larger antenna, providing a greater transmission range than handheld portable radios.

- Base station radios are located in fixed positions, such as dispatch centers, and tend to have the most powerful transmitters. A network is required to connect base stations to the same communication system.

- Repeaters increase the effective communication range of handheld portable radios, mobile radios, and base station radios by retransmitting received radio signals.

---

[8]Public safety officials include all emergency responders and public safety agencies, such as firefighters, police officers, and paramedics who are the first to arrive at the scene of an emergency, as well as other responders such as hospital personnel, who might not be on the scene of an emergency but are essential in supporting effective response and recovery operations. Public safety agencies include 911 call centers that are also essential in supporting an effective response.

Figure 1 illustrates the basic components of an LMR system.

Figure 1: Depiction of LMR System

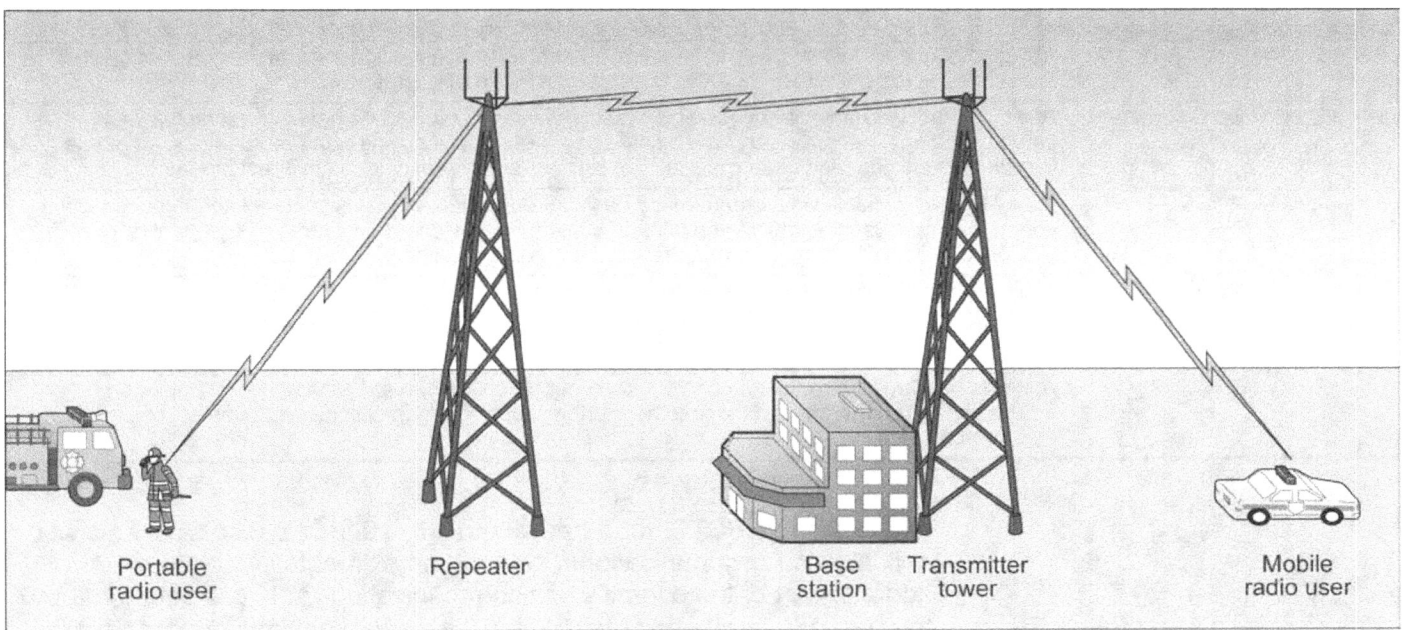

Portable radio user | Repeater | Base station | Transmitter tower | Mobile radio user

Source: GAO.

LMR systems are generally able to meet the unique requirements of public safety agencies. For example, unlike commercial cellular networks, which can allow seconds to go by before a call is set up and answered, LMR systems are developed to provide rapid voice call-setup and group-calling capabilities. When time is of the essence, as is often the case when public safety agencies need to communicate, it is important to have access to systems that achieve fast call-set up times. Furthermore, LMR systems provide public safety agencies "mission critical" voice capabilities—that is, voice capabilities that meet a high standard for reliability, redundancy, capacity, and flexibility. Table 1 describes the key elements for mission critical voice capabilities, as determined by the National Public Safety Telecommunications Council (NPSTC).[9]

---

[9]NPSTC is a federation of organizations whose mission is to improve public safety communications and interoperability through collaborative leadership.

Table 1: Key Elements for Mission Critical Voice Capabilities

Key element	Description
Direct or talk around	Ability to communicate unit-to-unit when out of range of a wireless network or when working in a confined area; both the transmitter and receiver operate without support from infrastructure.
Push-to-talk	Ability to communicate instantly by pushing a button on the device to transmit a voice message. The speaker releases the button to return to a listening mode of operation.
Full duplex voice systems	Ability for multiple users to communicate (talk and listen) at the same time; for example, when communications are necessary with outside parties such as citizens with emergencies, language translation services, and other outside agencies providing service to an incident or event.
Group talk	Ability to communicate on a one-to-many basis. Group talk is of vital importance to the public safety community because it enables a speaker to simultaneously communicate to every member of a group, such as all firefighters in the interior of a burning building.
Talker identification	Ability to identify who is speaking at any given time.
Emergency alerting	Ability to communicate that a life-threatening condition has been encountered and that immediate access to the system is required.
High quality audio	Ability to hear audio in adverse conditions without repetition of the message; for example, an emergency responder must be able to hear prime voice communications regardless of background noises, such as a siren.

Source: GAO based on NPSTC information.

According to NPSTC, for a network to fully support public safety mission critical voice communications, each of the elements in table 1 must address part of the overall voice communications services supported by the network. In other words, NPSTC believes a network cannot be a mission critical network without all of these elements. Furthermore, unlike commercial networks, mission critical communication systems rely on "hardened" infrastructure, meaning that tower sites and equipment have been designed to provide reliable communications even in the midst of natural or man-made disasters. To remain operable during disasters, mission critical communications infrastructure requires redundancy, back-up power, and fortification against environmental stressors such as extremes of temperature and wind.

Nationwide, there are approximately 55,000 public safety agencies. These state and local agencies typically receive a license from FCC to operate and maintain their LMR voice systems. Since these systems are supported by state and local revenues, the agencies generally purchase equipment and devices using their own local budgets without always coordinating their actions with nearby agencies, which can hinder interoperability. Since 1989, public safety associations have collaborated with federal agencies to establish common technical standards for LMR systems and devices called Project 25 (P25). The purpose of these technical standards is to support interoperability between different LMR systems, that is, to enable seamless communication across public safety agencies and jurisdictions. While the P25 suite of standards is intended to promote interoperability by making public safety systems and devices compatible regardless of the manufacturer, it is a voluntary standard and currently incomplete.[10] As a result, many LMR devices manufactured for public safety are not compatible with devices made by rival manufacturers, which can undermine interoperability.

The federal government plays an important role in public safety communications by providing funding for emergency communication systems and working to increase interoperable communication systems. Congress, in particular, has played a critical role by designating radio frequency spectrum for public safety use. Furthermore, Congress can direct action by federal agencies and others in support of public safety. For example, through the Homeland Security Act of 2002, Congress established DHS and required the department, among other things, to develop a comprehensive national incident management system comprising all levels of government and to consolidate existing federal government emergency response plans into a single, coordinated national response plan.[11]

In its regulatory role, FCC licenses all public safety spectrum for state, local, and regional communication networks across the country. This includes more than 134,000 licenses for current public safety LMR narrowband communication systems and the single nationwide public safety broadband license.[12] As part of the digital television transition, Congress, under the Balanced Budget Act of 1997, mandated that FCC allocate 24 MHz of spectrum for public safety use.[13] FCC divided the 24 MHz by assigning 12 MHz for public safety narrowband use and 10 MHz

---

[10]The P25 suite of standards contains 8 open interfaces that exist between the various components of an LMR system. According to a PSCR official, of the 8 interfaces, only about 1.5 were complete at the time of our report.

[11]Homeland Security Act of 2002, Pub. L. No. 107-296, §502(5) and (6),116 Stat. 2135, 2212 (2002).

[12]The number of licenses excludes the 700 MHz public safety broadband license, the 4.9 GHz band, and public safety point-to-point microwave licenses.

[13]Pending legislation, the Middle Class Tax Relief and Job Creation Act of 2012, increases the amount of spectrum FCC is required to allocate for public safety from 24 to 34 MHz.

for public safety broadband use.[14] In September 2006, FCC established its Public Safety and Homeland Security Bureau (PSHSB), which is responsible for developing, recommending, and administering FCC's policies pertaining to public safety communications issues. FCC has issued a series of orders and proposed rulemakings and adopted rules addressing how to develop a public safety broadband network, some of which are highlighted:

- In 2007, FCC adopted an order to create a nationwide broadband network with the 10 MHz of spectrum designated for a public safety broadband network and the adjacent 10 MHz of spectrum—the Upper 700 MHz D Block, or "D Block."[15] As envisioned by FCC, this nationwide network would be shared by public safety and a commercial provider and operated by a public/private partnership. However, when FCC presented the D Block for auction in 2008 under these conditions, it received no qualifying bids and thus was not licensed. Subsequently it was found that the lack of commercial interest in the D Block was due in part to uncertainty about how the public/private partnership would work.[16] Although many stakeholders and industry participants called for the D Block to be reallocated to public safety, an alternate view is that auctioning the D Block for commercial use would have generated revenues for the U.S. Treasury.[17] As noted previously, a provision in pending legislation, the Middle Class Tax Relief and Job Creation Act of 2012, reallocates the D Block to public safety.

- In 2007, FCC licensed the 10 MHz of spectrum that FCC assigned for public safety broadband use to the Public Safety Spectrum Trust (PSST), a nonprofit organization representing major national public safety associations. This 10 MHz of spectrum, located in the upper

---

[14]The remaining 2 MHz were used as guardbands to protect from unwanted interference. *Second Report and Order*, 22 FCC Rcd. 15289 (2007).

[15]Spectrum is divided into frequency bands, each having technical characteristics that affect electronic transmission in different ways. "Bandwidth" is related to the transmission capacity of a frequency band and both the bandwidth and the frequency band can be described in MHz.

[16]FCC issued two further notices of proposed rulemakings since it attempted to auction the D Block, and a final order has not been adopted.

[17]When FCC auctions spectrum, the proceeds are to be deposited in the U.S. Treasury. 49 U.S.C. §309(j)(8).

700 MHz band is adjacent to the spectrum allocated to public safety for LMR communications. As the licensee, the PSST's original responsibilities included representing emergency responders' needs for a broadband network and negotiating a network sharing agreement with the winner of the D Block auction. However, since the D Block was not successfully auctioned, FCC stayed the majority of the rules guiding the PSST.[18]

- In 2009, public safety entities began requesting waivers from FCC's rules to allow early deployment of broadband networks in the 10 MHz of spectrum licensed to the PSST, and since 2010, FCC granted waivers to 22 jurisdictions for early deployment.[19] These jurisdictions had to request waivers because the rules directing the deployment of a broadband network were not complete. In this report, we refer to the 22 entities receiving waivers as "waiver jurisdictions." As a condition of these waivers, FCC required that local or regional networks would interoperate with each other and that all public safety entities in the geographic area would be invited to use the new networks. In addition, FCC required that all equipment operating on the 700 MHz public safety broadband spectrum comply with Long Term Evolution (LTE), a commercial data standard for wireless technologies.[20] As shown in table 2, of the 22 jurisdictions that successfully petitioned for waivers, only 8 received federal funding. Seven waiver jurisdictions received funding from NTIA's Broadband Technology Opportunities Program (BTOP), a federal grant program authorized through the American Recovery and Reinvestment Act of 2009 that had several

---

[18] *Third Report and Order and Fourth Further Notice*, Service Rules for the 698-746, 747-762 and 777-792 Bands; Implementing a Nationwide, Broadband, Interoperable Public Safety Network in the 700 MHz Band, 26 FCC Rcd 733 (2011).

[19] *Requests for Waiver of Various Petitioners to Allow the Establishment of 700 MHz Interoperable Public Safety Wireless Broadband Networks*, Order, 25 FCC Rcd 5145, May 12, 2010; *Requests for Waiver of Various Petitioners to Allow the Establishment of 700 MHz Interoperable Public Safety Wireless Broadband Networks*, Order, 25 FCC Rcd 6783, May 12, 2011.

[20] LTE—the standard created and adopted by the Third Generation Partnership Project, a standards organization—is the closest standard to fourth generation wireless (4G) technology that existed at that time. LTE has been accepted and adopted by national and international communities as the foundation for future mobile telecommunications.

purposes, including promoting the expansion of broadband infrastructure.[21]

Table 2: Waiver Jurisdictions as of January 2012 and Federal Funds Provided for Public Safety Broadband Networks

Jurisdiction	Federal funds[a]	Source
Los Angeles Regional Interoperable Communications System (LA-RICS), California	$154.6 million	BTOP
Mississippi Wireless Communications Commission	70.1 million	BTOP
San Francisco, Oakland, and San Jose (BayWEB), California[b]	50.6 million	BTOP
New Jersey	39.6 million	BTOP
New Mexico	38.7 million	BTOP
Charlotte, North Carolina	16.7 million	BTOP
Adams County Communications Center, Colorado	12.1 million	BTOP
Texas	7.6 million	Port Security Grant
	750,000	Regional Catastrophic Planning Grant
Calumet, Outagamie and Winnebago counties, Wisconsin		
Boston, Massachusetts		
Chesapeake, Virginia		
Mesa, Arizona/TOPAZ Regional Wireless Cooperative		
New York, New York		
Pembroke Pines, Florida		
San Antonio, Texas		
Seattle, Washington		
District of Columbia		
Hawaii and various cities and counties		
Iowa		
New York		

[21]American Recovery and Reinvestment Act of 2009, Pub. L. No. 111-5, 123 Stat. 115 (2009).

Jurisdiction	Federal funds[a] Source
Oregon	
Alabama[c]	
Total	$390.8 million

Source: GAO analysis of FCC and NTIA data.

[a]This field appears empty for jurisdictions with no federal funds identified.

[b]Motorola, Inc., is the recipient of the BTOP funds used to build the BayWEB network.

[c]Alabama applied and was granted a waiver but did not execute a lease agreement with the PSST.

- In January 2011, FCC adopted rules and proposed further rules to create an effective technical framework for ensuring the deployment and operation of a nationwide, interoperable public safety broadband network.[22] As part of this proceeding, FCC sought comment on technical rules and security for the network as well as testing of equipment to ensure interoperability. The comment period for the proceeding closed on April 11, 2011, and FCC received comments from waiver jurisdictions, consultants, and manufacturers, among others. As of February 7, 2012, FCC did not have an expected issuance date for its final rules.

In addition to FCC, DHS has been heavily involved since its inception in supporting public safety by assisting federal, state, local, and regional emergency response agencies and policy makers with planning and implementing interoperable communication networks. Within DHS, several divisions have focused on improving public safety communications. DHS also has administered groups that bring together stakeholders from all levels of government to discuss interoperability issues:

- The Emergency Communications Preparedness Center (ECPC) was created in response to Hurricane Katrina by the 21st Century Emergency Communications Act of 2006 to help improve intergovernmental emergency communications information sharing.[23]

---

[22]FCC issued its *Third Report and Order and Fourth Further Notice of Proposed Rulemaking* in this proceeding. See, Service Rules for the 698-746, 747-762 and 777-792 Bands; Implementing a Nationwide, Broadband, Interoperable Public Safety Network in the 700 MHz Band; Amendment of Part 90 of the Commission Rules, *Third Report and Order and Fourth Notice of Proposed Rulemaking,* 23 FCC Rcd 14301 (2011).

[23]Pub. L. No.109-295, §671, 120 Stat.1433, 1440 (2006).

The ECPC has 14 member agencies with a goal, in part, to support and promote interoperable public safety communications through serving as a focal point and clearing house for information. It has served to facilitate collaboration across federal entities involved with public safety communications.

- SAFECOM is a communications program that provides support, including research and development, to address interoperable communications issues. Led by an executive committee, SAFECOM has members from state and local emergency responders as well as intergovernmental and national public safety communications associations. DHS draws on this expertise to help develop guidance and policy. Among other activities, SAFECOM publishes annual grant guidance that outlines recommended eligible activities and application requirements for federal grant programs providing funding for interoperable public safety communications.

Within Commerce, NTIA and NIST are also involved in public safety communications by providing research support to the PSCR program. The PSCR serves as a laboratory and advisor on public safety standards and technology. It provides research and development to help improve public safety interoperability. For example, the PSCR has ongoing research in many areas related to communications, including the voluntary P25 standard for LMR communication systems, improving public safety interoperability, and the standards and technologies related to a broadband network. PSCR also conducts laboratory research to improve the audio and video quality for public safety radios and devices.

Even With Investment of Significant Resources, Current Public Safety Communication Systems Provide Mission Critical Voice Capabilities but Are Not Fully Interoperable

Public Investment

Congress has appropriated billions in federal funding over the last decade to public safety in grants and other assistance for the construction and maintenance of LMR voice communication systems and the purchase of communication devices. Approximately 40 grant programs administered by nine federal agencies have provided this assistance for public safety.[24] Some of the grants provided a one-time infusion of funds, while other grants have provided a more consistent source of funding. For example, in 2007, the one-time Public Safety Interoperable Communications Grant Program awarded more than $960 million to assist state and local public safety agencies in the acquisition, planning, deployment, or training on interoperable communication systems.[25] However, the Homeland Security Grant Program has provided $6.5 billion since 2008, targeting a broad scope of programs that enhance interoperability for states' emergency medical response systems and regional communication systems, as well as planning at the community level to improve emergency preparedness. See appendix II for more information about the grant programs.

---

[24]Funding from these grants can support emergency communications; not all funding was spent on the LMR voice communication systems.

[25]The Public Safety Interoperable Communications Grant Program is an NTIA program administered by the Federal Emergency Management Agency.

State and local governments have also invested millions of dollars of their own funds to support public safety voice communications, and continue to do so. Jurisdictions we visited that received federal grants to support the construction of a broadband network have continued to invest in the upgrade and maintenance of their current LMR voice systems. For example, Adams County, Colorado, has spent about $19.7 million since 2004 on its LMR system, including $6.9 million in local funds, supplemented with $12.8 million in federal grants. Mississippi, another jurisdiction we visited that is constructing a statewide broadband network, has spent about $214 million on its LMR network, including $57 million in general revenue bonds and $157 million in federal grants.[26] Officials in the jurisdictions we contacted stressed the importance of investing in the infrastructure of their LMR networks to maintain the reliability and operability of their voice systems, since it was unclear at what point the broadband networks would support mission critical voice communications. In addition to upgrading and maintaining their LMR networks, many jurisdictions are investing millions of dollars to meet FCC's requirement that communities use their spectrum more efficiently by reducing the bandwidth on which they operate.[27]

In addition to direct federal funding, the federal government has allocated more than 100 MHz of spectrum to public safety over the last 60 years.[28] The spectrum is located in various frequency bands since FCC assigned frequencies to public safety in new bands over time as available frequencies became congested and public safety's need for spectrum increased.[29] Figure 2 displays the spectrum allocated to public safety, which is located between 25 MHz and 4.9 GHz. As noted previously, the Middle Class Tax Relief and Job Creation Act of 2012 requires FCC to reallocate the D Block from commercial use to public safety use.

---

[26]Mississippi retained a portion of the grant funds for administrative purposes.

[27]FCC requires that public safety LMR systems migrate to at least 12.5 kHz efficiency technology by January 1, 2013, in an effort to ensure more efficient use of the spectrum. 47 C.F.R. §90.209(b)(5), fn. 3.

[28]In comparison, FCC has licensed about 260 MHz of spectrum for broadband personal communication services through auctions, which are a market-based mechanism in which FCC assigns a license to the entity that submits the highest bid for specific bands of spectrum. Public safety has received spectrum outside of the auction process.

[29]Approximately half of this allocation is located at 4.9 GHz, which according to DHS has limited value to public safety. Ideal spectrum for public safety lies in the 150 to 800 MHz bands.

Figure 2: Current Allocation of Public Safety Spectrum

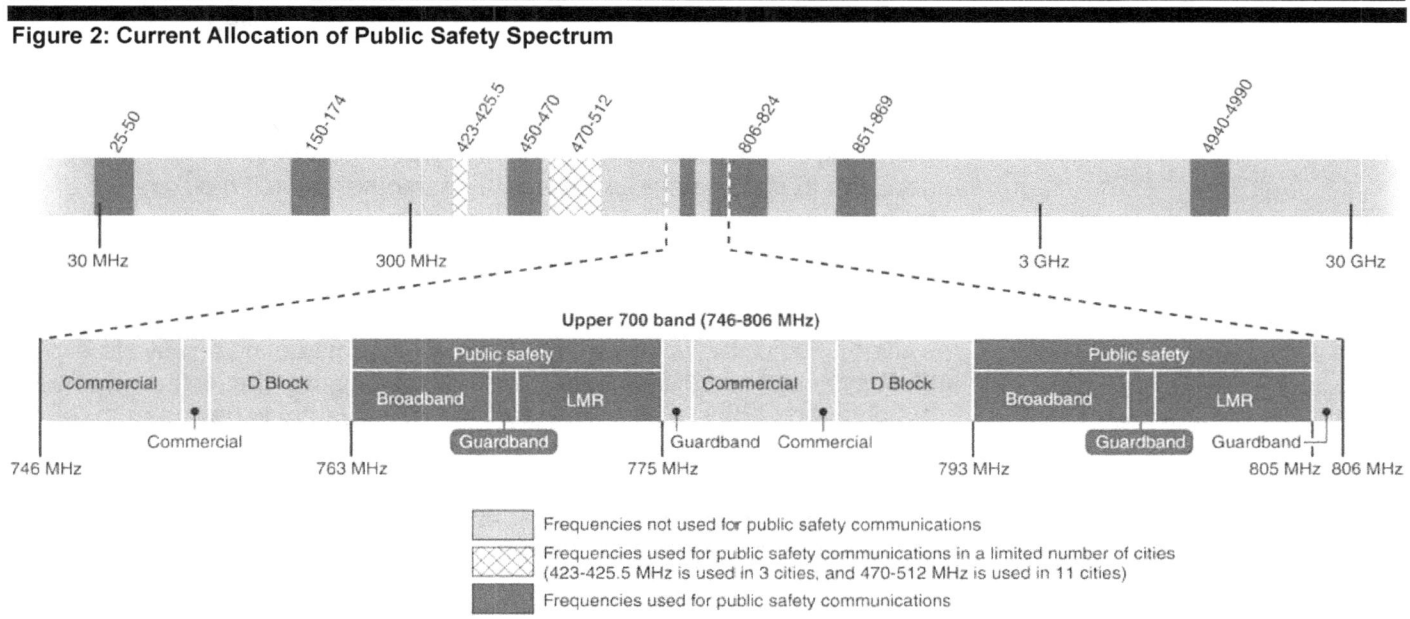

Frequencies not used for public safety communications

Frequencies used for public safety communications in a limited number of cities (423-425.5 MHz is used in 3 cities, and 470-512 MHz is used in 11 cities)

Frequencies used for public safety communications

Sources: GAO and FCC.

Public safety agencies purchase radios and communication devices that are designed to operate on their assigned frequency. Since different frequencies of radio waves have different propagation characteristics, jurisdictions typically use the spectrum that is best suited to their particular location. For example, very high frequency (VHF) channels—those located between 30 and 300 MHz—are more useful for communications that must occur over long distances without obstruction from buildings, since the signals cannot penetrate building walls very well. As such, VHF signals are well suited to rural areas. On the other hand, ultra high frequency (UHF) channels—those located between 300 MHz and 3 GHz—are more appropriate for denser urban areas as they have more capacity and can penetrate buildings more easily. When we visited Adams County, Colorado, we learned that public safety officials in the mountainous areas of Colorado use the 150 MHz and 450 MHz bands because of the range of the signals and their ability to navigate around the natural geography. However, public safety officials in the Denver, Colorado, metropolitan area operate on the 700 and 800 MHz frequency bands which can support more simultaneous voice transmissions, such as communications between fire, police, public utility, and transportation officials.

Current Public Safety Communications Capabilities

The current public safety LMR systems use their allocated spectrum to facilitate reliable mission critical voice communications. Such communications need to be conveyed in an immediate and clear manner regardless of environmental and other operating conditions. For example, while responding to a building fire, firefighters deep within the building need the ability to communicate with each other even if they are out of range of a wireless network. The firefighters are able to communicate on an LMR system because their handheld devices operate on as well as off network. Currently, emergency response personnel rely exclusively on their LMR systems to provide mission critical voice capabilities. One waiver jurisdiction we visited, Mississippi, is constructing a new statewide LMR system and officials there noted a high degree of satisfaction with the planned LMR system. They said the new system is designed to withstand most disasters and when complete, will provide interoperability across 97 percent of the state. Public safety officials in the coastal region of the state have already used the system to successfully respond to problems caused by the Mississippi River flooding in the spring of 2011.

LMR public safety communication systems also are able to provide some data services but the systems are constrained by the narrowband channels on which they operate. These channels allow only restricted data transfer speeds, thus limiting capacity to send and receive data such as text and images, or to access existing databases. Some jurisdictions supplement their LMR systems with commercial data services that give them better access to applications that require higher data transfer rates to work effectively. However, commercial service also has limitations, such as the lack of priority access to the network in an emergency situation.

Interoperability of Current Communication Systems Remains a Limitation

According to DHS, interoperability of current public safety communications has improved as a result of its efforts. In particular, the DHS National Emergency Communications Plan established a strategy for improving emergency communications across all levels of government, and as a result, all states have a statewide interoperability coordinator and governing body to make strategic decisions within the state and guide current and future communications interoperability. According to DHS, it has worked with states to help them evaluate and improve their emergency communications abilities. DHS also helped to develop the Interoperability Continuum, which identifies five critical success elements to assist emergency response agencies and policy makers to plan and implement interoperability solutions for data and voice communications. Furthermore, DHS created guidance to ensure a consistent funding strategy for federal grant programs that allow recipients to purchase communications equipment and enhance their emergency response capabilities. As we have reported in the past, interoperability has also improved due to a variety of local technical solutions.[30] For example, FCC established mutual aid channels, whereby specific channels are set aside for the sole purpose of connecting incompatible systems. Another local solution is when agencies maintain a cache of extra radios that they can distribute during an emergency to other first responders whose radios are not interoperable with their own.

However, despite decades of effort, a significant limitation of current LMR systems is that they are not fully interoperable. One reason for the lack of interoperability is the fragmentation of spectrum assignments for public safety, since existing radios are typically unable to transmit and receive in all these frequencies. Therefore, a rural area using public safety radios operating on VHF spectrum will not be interoperable with radios used in an urban area that operate on UHF spectrum. While radios can be built to operate on multiple frequencies, which could support greater interoperability, this capability can add significant cost to the radios and thus jurisdictions may be reluctant to make such investments. In addition, public safety agencies historically have acquired communication systems without concern for interoperability, often resulting in multiple, technically incompatible radio systems. This is compounded by the lack of mandatory standards for the current LMR systems or devices. Rather, the P25 technical standards remain incomplete and voluntary, creating incompatibility among vendors' products. Furthermore, local jurisdictions are often unable to coordinate to find solutions. Public safety communication systems are tailored to meet the unique needs of individual jurisdictions or public safety entities within a given region. As such, the groups are reluctant to give up management and control of their systems.

---

[30]GAO, *First Responders: Much Work Remains to Improve Communications Interoperability*, GAO-07-301 (Washington, D.C.: Apr. 2, 2007).

Planning for a Nationwide Public Safety Broadband Network Progresses, but Such a Network Will Not Support Mission Critical Voice for the Foreseeable Future

Federal Role

Numerous federal entities have helped to plan and begin to define a technical framework for a nationwide public safety broadband network. In particular, FCC, DHS, and Commerce's PSCR program, have coordinated their planning and made significant contributions by developing technical rules, educating emergency responders, and creating a demonstration network, respectively.

Since 2008, FCC has:

- Created a new division within its PSHSB, called the Emergency Response Interoperability Center (ERIC), to develop technical requirements and procedures to help ensure an operable and interoperable nationwide network.[31]

- Convened two advisory committees, the ERIC Technical Advisory Committee and the Public Safety Advisory Committee, that provide advice to FCC.[32] The Technical Advisory Committee's appointees must be federal officials, elected officers of state and local government, or a designee of an elected official. It makes

---

[31]Establishment of an Emergency Response Interoperability Center, PS Docket 06-229, *Order*, FCC 10-67 (rel. Apr. 23, 2010).

[32]The Public Safety Advisory Committee is subject to the Federal Advisory Committee Act; the Technical Advisory Committee is not. The Federal Advisory Committee Act regulates the creation, operation, and termination of executive branch advisory committees.

recommendations to FCC and ERIC regarding policies and rules for the technical aspects of interoperability, governance, authentication, and national standards for public safety. ERIC's Public Safety Advisory Committee's members can include representatives of state and local public safety agencies, federal users, and other segments of the public safety community, as well as service providers, equipment vendors, and other industry participants. Its purpose is to make recommendations for a technical framework that will ensure interoperability on a nationwide public safety broadband network.

- Defined technical rules for the broadband network, including identifying LTE as the technical standard for the network, which FCC and public safety agencies believe is imperative to the goal of achieving an interoperable nationwide broadband network. In addition, FCC sought comments on other technical aspects and challenges to building the network in its most recent proceeding, which FCC hopes will further promote and enable nationwide interoperability. FCC officials said they continue to monitor the waiver jurisdictions that are developing broadband networks to ensure they are meeting the network requirements by reviewing required reports and quarterly filings.

Since 2010, DHS has:

- Partnered with FCC, Commerce, and the Department of Justice to conduct three forums for public safety agencies and others. These forums provided insight about the needs surrounding the establishment of a public safety broadband network as they relate to funding, governance, and the broadband market.

- Coordinated federal efforts on broadband implementation by bringing together the member agencies of ECPC. Also, ECPC updated its grant guidance for federal grant programs to clarify that broadband deployment is an allowable expense for emergency communications grant programs. These updates could result in more federal grant funding going to support the development of a broadband network.

- Updated its SAFECOM program's grant guidance targeting grant applicants to include information pertaining to broadband deployment, based on input from state and local emergency responders.

- Worked with public safety entities to define the LTE standard and write educational materials about the broadband network.

- Partnered with state and regional groups and interoperability coordinators in preparing broadband guidance documentation.

- Represented federal emergency responders and advocated for sharing agreements between the federal government and the PSST that will enable federal users, such as responders from the Federal Emergency Management Agency, to access the broadband network.[33]

Since 2009, PSCR has:

- Worked with public safety agencies to develop requirements for the network and represents their interests before standards-setting organizations to help ensure public safety needs are met.

- Developed a demonstration broadband network that provides a realistic environment for public safety and industry to test and observe public safety LTE requirements on equipment designed for a broadband network. According to PSCR representatives, the demonstration network has successfully brought together more than 40 vendors, including manufacturers and wireless carriers. Among many goals, PSCR aims to demonstrate to public safety how the new technology can meet their needs and encourage vendors to share information and results. FCC requires the 22 waiver jurisdictions and their vendors to participate in PSCR's demonstration network and provide feedback on the challenges they have faced while building the network. PSCR representatives told us that the lessons learned from the waiver jurisdictions would be applied to future deployments.

- Tested interoperable systems and devices and provided feedback to manufacturers. Currently, there are five manufacturers working with PSCR to develop and test systems and devices.

Broadband Network Could Improve Incident Response

With higher data speeds than the current LMR systems, a public safety broadband network could provide emergency responders with new video and data applications that are not currently available. Stakeholders we contacted, including waiver jurisdictions, emergency responders, and

---

[33]Federal users are allowed to access the public safety broadband network, subject to the public safety broadband licensee's approval, 47 C.F.R. § 2.103(c)(1). FCC cannot license federal users, but federal users might be able to subscribe to the network.

federal agencies, identified transmission of video as a key potential capability. For example, existing video from traffic cameras and police car mounted cameras could provide live video feeds for dispatchers. Dispatchers could use the video to help ensure that the proper personnel and necessary equipment are being deployed immediately to the scene of an emergency. Stakeholders we contacted predict that numerous data applications will be developed once a broadband network is complete, and that these applications will have the potential to further enhance incident response. These could range from a global positioning system application that provides directions based on traffic patterns to a 3D graphical floor plan display that supports firefighters' efforts to battle building fires. In addition, unlike the current system, a public safety broadband network could provide access to existing databases of information, such as fire response plans and mug shots of wanted criminals, which could help to keep emergency responders and the public safe. As shown in figure 3, moving from lower bandwidth voice communications to a higher bandwidth broadband network unleashes the potential for the development of a range of public safety data applications.

Figure 3: Additional Emergency Response Capabilities from Increased Data Transfer Rates and Bandwidth

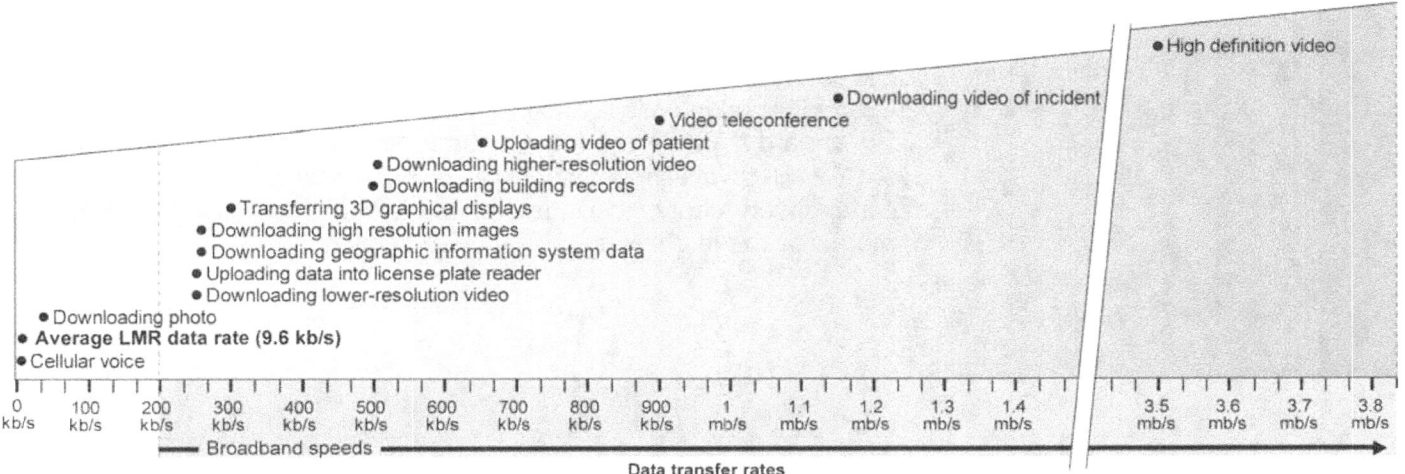

Source: GAO analysis.

Notes: The data transfer rates listed in this figure are estimates. Rates vary depending on whether data are uploaded or downloaded—typically, data are faster to download than to upload. Download speed is the speed of getting information from the Web to a computer or handheld device, and upload speed is the reverse. In addition, higher data transfer rates may be required when data are transmitted to or from a moving device or when a device is further from the tower transmitting the signal.

Kb/s means kilobit per second, and mb/s means megabit per second.

Besides new applications, a public safety broadband network has the potential to provide nationwide access and interoperability. Nationwide access means emergency responders and other public safety officials could access their home networks from anywhere in the country, which could facilitate a better coordinated emergency response. Interoperability on a broadband network could allow emergency responders to share information irrespective of jurisdiction or type of public safety agency. For example, officials from two waiver jurisdictions indicated that forest fires are a type of emergency that brings together multiple jurisdictions, and in these situations a broadband network could facilitate sharing of response plans. However, an expert we contacted stressed that broadband applications should be tailored to the bandwidth needs of the response task. For example, responders should not use high-definition video when grainy footage would suffice to enable them to pursue a criminal suspect.

Limitations of Broadband Results in Continued Reliance on LMR Voice Systems

A major limitation of a public safety broadband network is that it would not provide mission critical voice communications for many years. LTE, the standard FCC identified for the public safety broadband network, is a wireless broadband standard that is not currently designed to support mission critical voice communications. Commercial wireless providers are currently developing voice over LTE capabilities, but this will not meet public safety's mission critical voice requirements because key elements needed for mission critical voice, such as push-to-talk, are not part of the LTE standard.[34] While one manufacturer believes mission critical voice over LTE will be available as soon as 5 years, some waiver jurisdictions, experts, government officials, and others told us it will likely be 10 years or more due to the challenges described in table 3.

---

[34]The LTE standard is still being developed.

Table 3: Challenges to Developing Mission Critical Voice Capabilities for LTE

Key element for mission critical voice	Challenges for LTE
Direct or talk around	As the LTE standard is a commercial standard, it may not be in the financial interest of commercial providers to develop this capability.
Push-to-talk	Standards need to be developed for this technology and the technology needs to be able to connect and transmit with very little delay.
Group talk	Messages to groups will require bandwidth and the amount can vary based on the size of the group. The bandwidth for voice will take away from the bandwidth available for data.
High quality audio	Digital communications for radio networks have created challenges in the past and the new technology should allow a voice to be understood without repetition, as well as allow background noises to be heard without interference.

Source: GAO based on industry information.

Absent mission critical voice capabilities on a broadband network, emergency responders will continue to rely on their current LMR voice systems, meaning a broadband network would supplement, rather than replace, LMR systems for the foreseeable future. Furthermore, until mission critical voice communications exist, issues that exacerbated emergency response efforts to the terrorist attacks on September 11, 2001—in particular, that emergency responders were not able to communicate between agencies—will not be resolved by a public safety broadband network. As a result, public safety agencies will continue to use devices operating on the current LMR systems for mission critical voice communications, and require spectrum to be allocated for that purpose. Additionally, public safety agencies may be reluctant to give up their LMR devices, especially if they were costly and are still functional. As jurisdictions continue to spend millions of dollars on their LMR networks and devices, they will likely continue to rely on such communication systems until they are no longer functional.[35]

In addition to not having mission critical communications, emergency responders may only have limited access to the public safety broadband network from the interior of large buildings. While the 700 MHz spectrum provides better penetration of buildings than other bands of the spectrum, if emergency responders expect to have access to the network from inside large buildings and underground, additional infrastructure will need to be constructed. For example, antennas or small indoor cellular stations

---

[35]LMR devices typically operate for more than 10 years, much longer than the standard commercial device.

could be installed inside buildings and in underground structures to support access to the network. FCC is seeking comment on this issue as part of its most recent proceeding. Without this added infrastructure, emergency responders using the broadband network may not have access to building blue prints or fire response plans during building emergencies, such as a fire. In fact, one jurisdiction constructing a broadband network that we visited told us their network would not support in-building access in one city of the jurisdiction because the plan did not include antennas for inside the buildings.

A final limitation to a public safety broadband network could be its capacity during emergencies. Emergencies tend to happen in localized areas that may be served by a single cell tower or even a single cellular antenna on a tower.[36] With emergency responders gathering to fight a fire or other emergency, the number of responders and the types of applications in use may exceed the capacity of the network. If the network reaches capacity it could overload and might not send life saving information.[37] Therefore, the network would have to be managed during emergencies to ensure that the most important data are being sent, which could be accomplished by prioritizing data. Furthermore, capacity could be supplemented through deployable cell sites to emergency locations.

Various Challenges Could Jeopardize the Implementation and Functionality of a Public Safety Broadband Network

Although the federal agencies have taken important steps to advance the broadband network, challenges exist that may slow its implementation. Specifically, stakeholders we spoke with prioritized five challenges to successfully building, operating, and maintaining a public safety broadband network. These challenges include (1) ensuring interoperability, (2) creating a governance structure, (3) building a reliable network, (4) designing a secure network, and (5) determining funding sources. FCC, in its *Fourth Further Notice of Proposed Rulemaking*, sought comment on some of these challenges, and as explained further, the challenge of creating a governance structure has been addressed by recent law. However, the other challenges currently remain unresolved

---

[36]The technical design of a cellular network involves multiple hexagonal shaped cells merging together to form the network.

[37]One waiver jurisdiction ran simulations on 10 MHz of 700 MHz spectrum and determined that when overloaded the network became unusable for video and data.

and, if left unaddressed, could undermine the development of a public safety broadband network.

Ensuring interoperability. To avoid a major shortcoming of the LMR communication systems, it is essential that a public safety broadband network be interoperable across jurisdictions and devices. DHS, in conjunction with its SAFECOM program, developed the Interoperability Continuum which identifies five key elements to interoperable networks— governance, standard operating procedures, technology, training, and usage—that waiver jurisdictions and other stakeholders discussed as important to building an interoperable public safety broadband network, as shown in figure 4. For example, technology is critical to interoperability of the broadband network and most stakeholders, including public safety associations, experts, and manufacturers believe that identifying LTE as the technical standard was a good step towards interoperability. To further promote interoperability, stakeholders indicated that additional technical functionality, such as data sharing and roaming capabilities, should be part of the technical design. If properly designed to the technical standard, broadband devices will support interoperability regardless of the manufacturer. Testing devices to ensure they meet the identified standard could help eliminate devices with proprietary applications that might otherwise limit interoperability. In its Fourth Further Notice, FCC solicited input on the technical design of the network and testing of devices to ensure interoperability.[38]

---

[38]Pending legislation, the Middle Class Tax Relief and Job Creation Act of 2012, requires the creation of a Technical Advisory Board for First Responder Interoperability to develop recommended minimum technical requirements to ensure a nationwide level of interoperability.

Figure 4: SAFECOM Interoperability Continuum with Five Key Elements

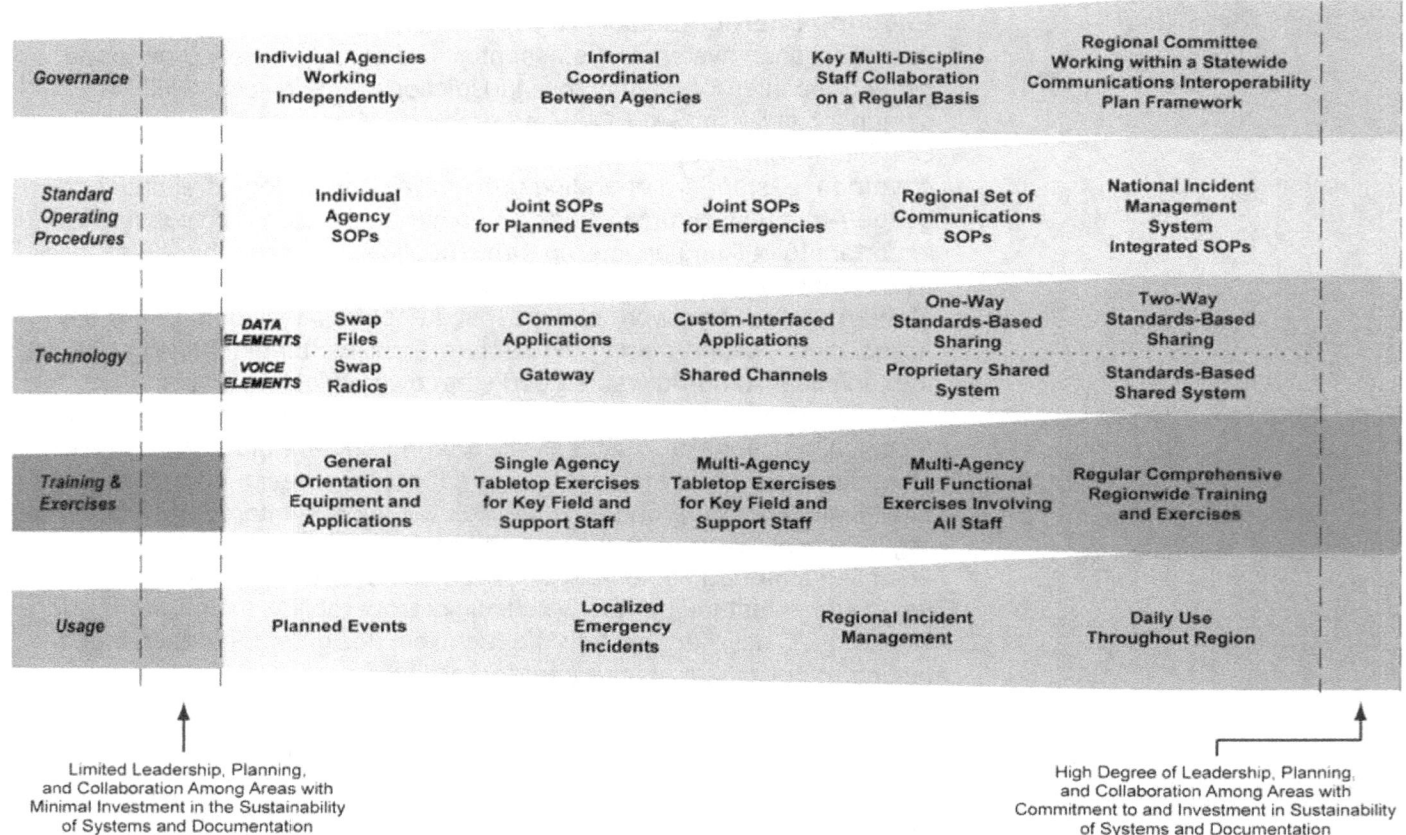

Source: SAFECOM

Note: This graphic was created by DHS in conjunction with its SAFECOM program and we made a minor revision to its appearance.

Creating a governance structure. As stated previously, governance is a key element for interoperable networks. A governance authority can promote interoperability by bringing together federal, state, local, and emergency response representatives. Each of the waiver jurisdictions we contacted had identified a governance authority to oversee its broadband network. Jurisdictions we visited, as well as federal agencies, told us that any nationwide network should also have a nationwide governance entity to oversee it. Although several federal entities are involved with the planning of a public safety broadband network, at the time we conducted our work no entity had overall authority to make critical decisions for its development, construction, and operation. According to stakeholders, decisions on developing a common language for the network, establishing user rights for federal agencies, and determining network upgrades, could be managed by such an entity. Pending legislation, the Middle Class Tax Relief and Job Creation Act of 2012, establishes a First Responder Network Authority as an independent authority within NTIA and gave it responsibility for ensuring the establishment of a nationwide, interoperable public safety broadband network. Among other things, the First Responder Network Authority is required to (1) ensure nationwide standards for use and access of the network; (2) issue open, transparent, and competitive requests for proposals to private sector entities to build, operate, and maintain the network; (3) encourage that such requests leverage existing commercial wireless infrastructure to speed deployment of the network; and (4) manage and oversee the implementation and execution of contracts and agreements with nonfederal entities to build, operate, and maintain the network.

Building a reliable network. A public safety broadband network must be as reliable as the current LMR systems but it will require additional infrastructure to do so. As mentioned previously, emergency responders consider the current LMR systems very reliable, in part because they can continue to work in emergency situations. Any new broadband network would need to meet similar standards but, as shown in figure 5, such a network might require up to 10 times the number of towers as the current system. This is because a public safety broadband network is being designed as a cellular network, which would use a series of low powered towers to transmit signals and reduce interference. Also, to meet robust public safety standards, each tower must be "hardened" to ensure that it can withstand disasters, such as hurricanes and earthquakes. According to waiver jurisdictions and other stakeholders, this additional infrastructure and hardening of facilities may be financially prohibitive for many jurisdictions, especially those in rural areas that currently use devices operating on VHF spectrum—spectrum that is especially well suited to rural areas because the signals can travel long distances.

Figure 5: Example of Infrastructure Required for Current LMR Systems and a Public Safety Broadband Network

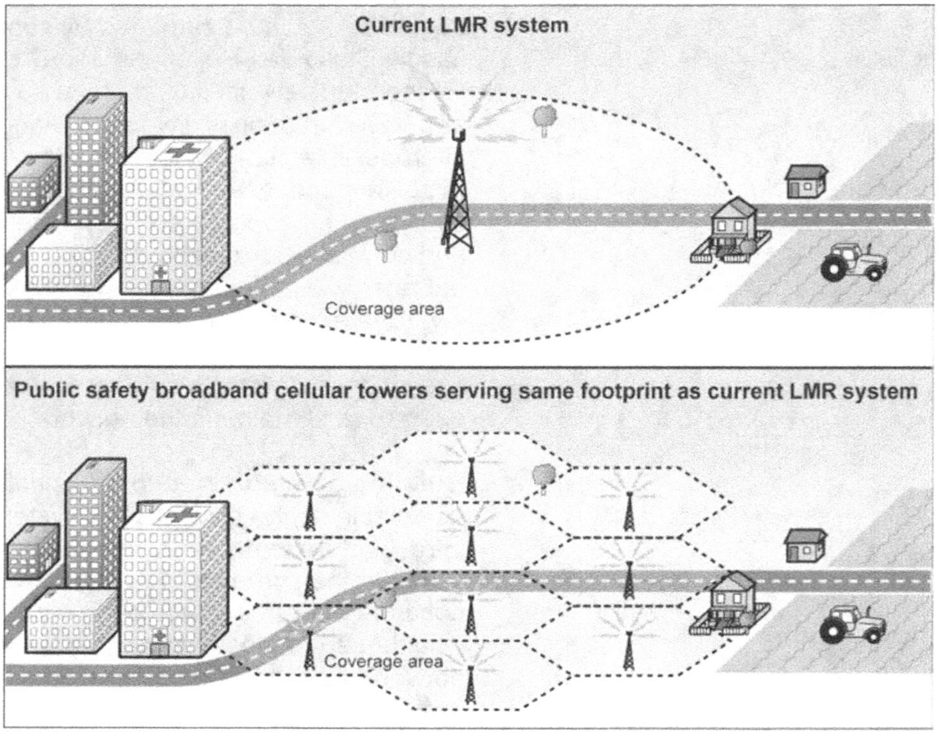

Source: GAO.

Note: The number of towers needed for a cellular network is dependent on the amount of spectrum used by the network and the reliability needed.

Designing a secure network. Secure communications are important. Designing a protected and trusted broadband network will encourage increased usage and reliance on it. Security for a public safety network will require authentication and access control. By defining LTE as the technical standard for the broadband network, a significant portion of the security architecture is predetermined because the standard governs a certain level of security. Given the importance of this issue, FCC required waiver jurisdictions to include some security features in their networks and FCC's most recent proceeding seeks input on security issues. Furthermore, FCC's Public Safety Advisory Committee has issued a report making several security-related recommendations. For example, it recommended that standardized security features be in place to support roaming to commercial technologies. However, one expert we contacted expressed concern that the waiver jurisdictions were not establishing sufficient network security because they had not received guidance. He believes this would result in waiver jurisdictions using security standards applied to previous networks.

Determining funding sources. It is estimated that a nationwide public safety broadband network could cost up to $15 billion or more to construct, which does not take into account recurring operation and maintenance costs.[39] As noted previously, of the 22 waiver jurisdictions, 8 have received federal grants to support deployment of a broadband network. Some of the other waiver jurisdictions have obtained limited funding from nonfederal sources, such as through issuing bonds. Several of the jurisdictions we spoke with stressed that in addition to the upfront construction costs, the ongoing costs associated with operating, maintaining, and upgrading a public safety broadband network would need to be properly funded. As previously indicated, the ECPC and SAFECOM have updated grant guidance to reflect changing technologies but this does not add additional funding for emergency communications. Rather, it defines broadband as an allowable purpose for emergency communications funding grants that may currently support the existing LMR systems. Since the LMR systems will not be replaced by a public safety broadband network, funding will be necessary to operate, maintain, and upgrade two separate communication systems.

Limited Competition and High Manufacturing Costs Increase the Price of Handheld LMR Devices, but Options Exist to Reduce Prices

---

[39]Pending legislation, the Middle Class Tax Relief and Job Creation Act of 2012, authorizes proceeds ($7 billion) from incentive auctions to construct the public safety network and authorizes the First Responder Network Authority to assess and collect fees to enable the authority to recoup its total expenses annually.

Competition for Handheld LMR Devices is Limited

Handheld LMR devices often cost thousands of dollars, and many stakeholders, including national public safety associations, state and local public safety officials, and representatives from the telecommunications industry, attribute these high prices to limited competition. Industry analysts and stakeholders estimate that the approximately $4 billion U.S. market for handheld LMR devices consists of one manufacturer with about 75 to 80 percent market share, one or two strong competitors, and several device manufacturers with smaller shares of the market.[40] According to industry stakeholders, competition is weak because of limited entry by device manufacturers; this may be due to (1) the market's relatively small size and (2) barriers to entry that confront nonincumbent device manufacturers.

Small size of the public safety market. The market for handheld LMR devices in the United States includes only about 2 to 3 million customers, or roughly 1 percent of the approximately 300 million customers of commercial telecommunication devices. According to an industry estimate in 2009, approximately 300,000 handheld LMR devices that are P25 compliant are sold each year. Annual sales of handheld LMR devices are small in part because of low turnover. For example, device manufacturers told us that public safety devices are typically replaced every 10 to 15 years, suggesting that less than 10 percent of handheld LMR devices are replaced annually. In contrast, industry and public safety sources indicate that commercial customers replace devices roughly every 2 to 3 years, suggesting that about 33 to 50 percent are replaced annually. Together, low device turnover and a small customer base reduce the potential volume of sales by device manufacturers, which may make the market unattractive to potential entrants.

The size of the market is reduced further by the need for manufacturers to customize handheld LMR devices for individual public safety agencies. Differences in spectrum allocations across jurisdictions have the effect of decreasing the customer base for any single device. As previously discussed, public safety agencies operate on different frequencies scattered across the radio spectrum. For example, one jurisdiction may need devices that operate on 700 MHz frequencies, whereas another

---

[40]The competitiveness of a market may be determined by factors other than the number of manufacturers within it—a market with only one manufacturer may be competitive if the manufacturer faces a credible threat of entry by competitors because the possibility that competitors will take away customers is enough to keep prices down.

jurisdiction may need devices that operate on both 800 MHz and 450 MHz frequencies. Existing handheld LMR devices typically do not transmit and receive signals in all public safety frequencies. As a result, device manufacturers cannot sell a single product to customers nationwide, and must tailor devices to the combinations of frequencies in use by the purchasing agency.

Barriers to entry by nonincumbent manufacturers. Device manufacturers wishing to enter the handheld LMR device market face barriers in doing so, which further limits competition. The use of proprietary technologies represents one barrier to entry. The inclusion of proprietary technologies often makes LMR devices noninteroperable with one another. This lack of interoperability makes it costly for customers to switch the brand of their devices, since doing so requires them to replace or modify older devices. These switching costs may continually compel customers to buy devices from the incumbent device manufacturer, preventing less established manufacturers from making inroads into the market. For example, in a comment filed with FCC, one of the jurisdictions we visited said that device manufacturers offer a proprietary encryption feature for free or at only a nominal cost.[41] When a public safety agency buys devices that incorporate this proprietary encryption feature, the agency cannot switch its procurement to a different manufacturer without undertaking costly modifications to its existing fleet of devices. Switching costs are particularly high when a device manufacturer has installed a communication system that is incompatible with competitors' devices. In this scenario, a public safety agency cannot switch to a competitor's handheld device without incurring the cost of new equipment or a patching mechanism to resolve the incompatibility. Even where devices from different manufacturers are compatible, a fear of incompatibility may deter agencies from switching to a nonincumbent brand. According to industry stakeholders—and as we have confirmed in the past—devices marketed as P25 compliant often are not interoperable in practice.[42] This lack of confidence in the P25 standard may encourage agencies to continue buying handheld LMR devices from their current

---

[41]Encryption features convert data into a code to prevent unauthorized access. Although the P25 standard permits certain encryption features in handheld LMR devices, some device manufacturers sell encryption technology that falls outside the P25 standard.

[42]GAO-07-301.

brand, placing less established device manufacturers at a disadvantage and thus discouraging competition.

At the same time that less established manufacturers are at a disadvantage, the market leader enjoys distinct "incumbency advantages." These advantages refer to the edge that a manufacturer derives from its position as incumbent, over and above whatever edge it derives from the strength of its product:

- According to an industry analyst, some public safety agencies are reluctant to switch brands of handheld LMR devices because their emergency responders are accustomed to the placement of the buttons on their existing devices.

- According to another industry analyst, the extensive network of customer representatives that the market leader has established over time presents an advantage. According to this analyst, less established device manufacturers face difficulty winning contracts because their networks of representatives are comparatively thin.

- The well-recognized brand of the market leader also represents an advantage. According to one stakeholder, some agencies mistakenly believe that only the market leader is able to manufacturer devices compliant with P25, and thus conduct sole-source procurements with this manufacturer. Even where procurements are competitive, the market leader is likely to enjoy an upper hand over its competitors; according to an industry analyst, local procurement officers prefer to buy handheld LMR devices from the dominant device manufacturer because doing so is an uncontroversial choice in the eyes of their management.[43]

High Manufacturing Costs and Lack of Buying Power Increase Device Prices

Competition aside, handheld LMR devices are costly to manufacture, so their prices will likely exceed prices for commercial devices regardless of how much competition exists in the market. First, this is in large part because these devices need to be reinforced for high-pressure environments. Handheld LMR devices must be able to withstand

[43]Further, incumbency advantages may be apparent in the standards development process. Stakeholders told us that because device manufacturers participate in the standards development process, the technology standards for handheld LMR devices may reflect the interests of dominant device manufacturers.

extremes of temperature as well physical stressors such as dust, smoke, impact, and immersion in water. Second, they also have much more robust performance requirements than commercial devices—including greater transmitter and battery power—to enable communication at greater ranges and during extended periods of operation. Third, the devices are produced in quantities too small to realize the cost savings of mass production. Manufacturers of commercial telecommunication devices can keep prices lower simply because of the large quantities they produce. For example, one industry stakeholder told us that economies of scale begin for commercial devices when a million or more devices are produced per manufacturing run. In contrast, LMR devices are commonly produced in manufacturing runs of 25,000 units. Fourth, the exterior of handheld LMR devices must be customized to the needs of emergency responders. For example, the buttons on these devices must be large enough to press while wearing bulky gloves.

In addition, given that the P25 standard remains incomplete and voluntary, device manufacturers develop products based on conflicting interpretations of the standard, resulting in incompatibilities between their products. Stakeholders from one jurisdiction we visited said that agencies can request add-on features—such as the ability to arrange channels according to user preference or to scan for radio channels assigned for particular purposes—which fall outside the P25 standard. These features increase the degree of customization required to produce handheld LMR devices, pushing costs upward.

Furthermore, public safety agencies may be unable to negotiate lower prices for handheld LMR devices because they cannot exert buying power in relationship with device manufacturers. We found that public safety agencies are not in an advantageous position to negotiate lower prices because they often request customized features and negotiate with device manufacturers in isolation from one another. According to a public safety official in one jurisdiction we contacted, each agency has unique ordinances, purchasing mechanisms, and bidding processes for devices. Because public safety agencies contract for handheld LMR devices in this independent manner, they sacrifice the quantity discounts that come from placing larger orders. Moreover, they are unlikely to know what other agencies pay for similar devices, enabling device manufacturers to offer different prices to different jurisdictions rather than set a single price for the entire market. One public safety official told us that small jurisdictions therefore pay more than larger jurisdictions for similar devices. As we have reported in the past, agencies that require similar products can combine their market power—and therefore obtain lower prices—by engaging in joint procurement.[44] Therefore, wider efforts to coordinate procurement at the state, regional, or national level are likely to increase the buying power of public safety agencies and help bring down prices.

Although these factors drive up prices in the current market for handheld LMR devices, industry observers said that many of these factors diminish in the future market for handheld broadband devices. As described earlier, FCC has mandated a commercial standard, LTE, for devices operating on the new broadband networks. The use of this standard may reduce the prevalence of proprietary features that inhibit interoperability. In addition, the new broadband networks will operate on common 700 MHz spectrum across the nation, eliminating the need to customize devices to the frequencies in use by individual jurisdictions. Together, the adoption of a commercial standard and the use of common spectrum are likely to increase the uniformity of handheld public safety devices, which in turn is likely to strengthen competition and enable the cost savings that come from bulk production. In addition, industry analysts and federal officials told us that they expect a heightened level of competition in the market for LTE devices because multiple device manufacturers are expected to develop them.

Options Exist to Reduce the Prices of Handheld LMR Devices

Options exist to reduce prices in the market for handheld LMR devices by increasing competition and the bargaining power of public safety agencies. One option is to reduce barriers to entry into the market. As described above, less established manufacturers may be discouraged from entering the market for handheld LMR devices because of the lack of interoperability between devices produced by different manufacturers. Consistent implementation of the P25 standard would increase interoperability between devices, enabling public safety agencies to mix and match handheld LMR devices from different brands. As we have reported in the past, independent testing is necessary to ensure compliance with standards and interoperability among products.[45] In the past several years, NIST and DHS have established a Compliance

---

[44]GAO, *Transit Rail: Potential Rail Car Cost-Saving Strategies Exist*, GAO-10-730 (Washington, D.C.: June 30, 2010), and GAO, *DOD and VA Pharmacy: Progress and Remaining Challenges in Jointly Buying and Mailing Out Drugs*, GAO-01-588 (Washington, D.C.: May 25, 2001).

[45]GAO, *Information Assurance: National Partnership Offers Benefits, but Faces Considerable Challenges*, GAO-06-392 (Washington, D.C.: Mar. 24, 2006).

Assessment Program (CAP) for the P25 standard. CAP provides a government-led forum in which to test devices for conformance with P25 specifications.[46] If the CAP program succeeds in increasing interoperability, it may reduce switching costs—that is, the expense of changing manufacturers—and thus may open the door to greater competition. Although CAP is a promising means to lower costs in this way, it is too soon to assess its effectiveness.

A second option is for public safety agencies to engage in joint procurement to lower costs. Joint procurement of handheld LMR devices could increase the bargaining power of agencies as well as facilitate cost savings through quantity discounts. One public safety official we interviewed said that while local agencies seek to maintain control over operational matters—such as which emergency responders operate on which channels—they are likely to cede control in procurement matters if doing so lowers costs.[47] As described earlier in this report, DHS provides significant grant funding, technical assistance, and guidance to enhance the interoperability of LMR systems. For example, as described in its January 2012 Technical Assistance Catalog, DHS's Office of Emergency Communications supports local public safety entities to ensure that LMR design documents meet P25 specifications and are written in a vendor-neutral manner. Based on its experience in emergency communications and its outreach to local public safety representatives, DHS is positioned to facilitate and incentivize opportunities for joint procurement of handheld LMR devices.

Conclusions

Despite their interoperability limitations, traditional LMR systems have provided public safety agencies with mission critical voice capabilities that commercial broadband systems cannot provide. These LMR systems will continue to be essential for public safety communications until broadband systems are able to meet public safety requirements, particularly for

---

[46]According to DHS, equipment that is found compliant is posted to the Responder Knowledge Base at (last accessed, Feb. 17, 2012) https://www.rkb.us/.

[47]An alternative approach to fostering joint procurement is through a federal supply schedule. In 2008, the Local Preparedness Acquisition Act, Pub. L. No. 110-248, 122 Stat. 2316 (2008), gave state and local governments the opportunity to buy emergency response equipment through GSA's Cooperative Purchasing Program. The Cooperative Purchasing Program may provide a model for extending joint procurement to state and local public safety agencies.

mission critical voice. As a result, a public safety broadband network would likely supplement, rather than replace, current LMR systems for the foreseeable future. Although a public safety broadband network could enhance incident response, it would have limitations and be costly to construct. Furthermore, since the LMR systems will still be operational for many years, funding will be necessary to operate, maintain, and upgrade two separate public safety communication systems.

At the time of our work, there was not an administrative entity that had the authority to plan, oversee, or direct the public safety broadband spectrum. As a result, overarching management decisions had not been made to guide the development or deployment of a public safety broadband network. According to SAFECOM's interoperability continuum, governance structures provide a framework for collaboration and decision making with the goal of achieving a common objective and therefore foster greater interoperability. In addition to ensuring interoperability, a governance entity with proper authority could help to address the challenges identified in this report, such as ensuring the network is secure and reliable. Pending legislation, the Middle Class Tax Relief and Job Creation Act of 2012, establishes an independent authority within NTIA to manage and oversee the implementation of a nationwide, interoperable public safety broadband network.

Handheld communication devices used by public safety officials can cost thousands of dollars, mostly due to limited competition and high manufacturing costs. However, public safety agencies also lack buying power vis-à-vis the device manufacturers, which may result in the agencies overpaying for the devices. In particular, since public safety agencies negotiate individually with device manufacturers, they are unlikely to know what other agencies pay for comparable devices and they sacrifice the increased bargaining power and economies of scale that accompany joint purchasing. Especially in rural areas, public safety agencies may be overpaying for handheld devices. We have repeatedly recommended joint procurement as a cost saving measure for situations where agencies require similar products because it allows them to combine their market power and lower their procurement costs. Given that DHS has expertise in emergency communications and relationships with local public safety representatives, we believe it is well-suited to facilitate opportunities for joint procurement of handheld communication devices.

Recommendation for Executive Action

To help ensure that public safety agencies are not overpaying for handheld communication devices, the Secretary of Homeland Security should work with federal and state partners to identify and communicate opportunities for joint procurement of public safety LMR devices.

Agency Comments and Our Evaluation

We provided a draft of this report to Commerce, DHS, the Department of Justice, and FCC for their review and comment. In the draft report we sent to the agencies, we included a matter for congressional consideration for ensuring that a public safety broadband network has adequate direction and oversight, such as by creating a governance structure that gives authority to an entity to define rules and develop a plan for the overarching management of the network. As a result of pending legislation that addresses this issue, we removed the matter for congressional consideration from the final report.

Commerce provided written comments, reprinted in appendix III, in which it noted that NIST and NTIA will continue to collaborate with and support state, local, and tribal public safety agencies and other federal agencies to help achieve effective and efficient public safety communications.

In commenting on the draft report, DHS concurred with our recommendation that it should work with federal and state partners to identify and communicate opportunities for joint procurement of public safety LMR devices While DHS noted that this recommendation will not likely assist near-term efforts to implement a public safety broadband network, assisting efforts for the broadband network was not the intention of the recommendation. Rather, we intended this recommendation to help ensure that public safety agencies do not overpay for handheld LMR devices by encouraging joint procurement. DHS suggested in response to our recommendation that a GSA solution may be more appropriate than DHS contracting activity. Although we recognize that a GSA solution is one possibility for joint procurement of handheld LMR devices, other opportunities and solutions might exist. We believe DHS, based on its experience in emergency communications and its outreach to state and local public safety representatives, is best suited to identify such opportunities and solutions for joint procurement and communicate those to the public safety agencies. In its letter, DHS also noted that it continues to work with federal, state, local, and private-sector partners to facilitate the deployment of a nationwide public safety broadband network, and stressed that establishing an effective governance structure is crucial to ensuring interoperability and effective use of the network. DHS's written comments are reprinted in appendix IV.

Commerce, DHS, the Department of Justice, and FCC provided technical comments on the draft report, which we incorporated as appropriate.

We are sending copies of this report to the Secretary of Homeland Security, the Attorney General, the Secretary of Commerce, the Chairman of FCC, and appropriate congressional committees. In addition, the report will be available at no charge on the GAO website at http://www.gao.gov.

If you or your staff have any questions about this report, please contact me at (202) 512-2834 or goldsteinm@gao.gov. Contact points for our Offices of Congressional Relations and Public Affairs may be found on the last page of this report. Contact information and major contributors to this report are listed on appendix V.

Mark L. Goldstein
Director, Physical Infrastructure

List of Requesters

The Honorable Fred Upton
Chairman
The Honorable Henry A. Waxman
Ranking Member
Committee on Energy and Commerce
House of Representatives

The Honorable John D. Rockefeller IV
Chairman
The Honorable Kay Bailey Hutchison
Ranking Member
Committee on Commerce, Science,
 and Transportation
United States Senate

The Honorable Greg Walden
Chairman
The Honorable Anna G. Eshoo
Ranking Member
Subcommittee on Communications and Technology
Committee on Energy and Commerce
House of Representatives

The Honorable Edward J. Markey
House of Representatives

Appendix I: Objectives, Scope, and Methodology

This report examines current communication systems used by public safety and issues surrounding the development of a nationwide public safety broadband network. Specifically, we reviewed (1) the resources that have been provided for current public safety communication systems and their capabilities and limitations, (2) how a nationwide public safety broadband network is being planned and its anticipated capabilities and limitations, (3) the challenges to building a nationwide public safety broadband network, and (4) the factors that influence competition and cost in the development of public safety communication devices and the options that exist to reduce prices.

To address all objectives, we conducted a literature review of 43 articles from governmental and academic sources on public safety communications. We reviewed these articles and recorded relevant evidence in workpapers, which informed our report findings. To identify existing studies, we conducted searches of various databases, such as EconLit, ProQuest, Academic OneFile, and Social SciSearch. We also pursued a snowball technique—following citations from relevant articles—to find other relevant articles and asked external researchers that we interviewed to recommend additional studies. These research methods produced 106 articles for initial review. We vetted this initial list by examining summary level information about each piece of literature, giving preference to articles that appeared in peer-reviewed journals and were germane to our research objectives. As a result, the 43 studies that we selected for our review met our criteria for relevance and quality. For the 13 articles related to our fourth objective—factors that affect competition and cost in the market for public safety communication devices—a GAO economist performed a secondary review and confirmed the relevance to our objective. Articles were then reviewed and evidence captured in workpapers. The workpapers were then reviewed for accuracy of the evidence gathered. We performed these searches and identified articles from June 2011 to September 2011.

We also interviewed government officials or stakeholders in 6 of the 22 jurisdictions that are authorized to build early public safety broadband networks and obtained information concerning each objective. In particular, we obtained information concerning their current communication systems and its capabilities, including any funding received to support the current network. We discussed their plan for building a public safety broadband network and the challenge they had faced thus far, including the role each thought the federal government should play in developing a network. We also discussed their views on the communication device market and the factors shaping the market. We selected jurisdictions to contact based on three criteria: (1) whether the jurisdiction received grant funds from the National Telecommunications and Information Administration (NTIA) to help build the network, (2) whether the planned network would be a statewide or regional network, and (3) geographic distribution across the nation. Table 4 lists the jurisdictions we selected based on these criteria. We selected jurisdictions based on NTIA grant funding because these jurisdictions had received the most significant federal funds dedicated towards developing a broadband network. Other jurisdictions either had not identified any funding or applied smaller grant funding that was not primarily targeted at emergency communications. We selected the size of the network, statewide or regional, to determine if challenges differed based on the size of the network and the number of entities involved. Finally, we selected sites based on the geographic region to get a geographic mix of jurisdictions from around the country. In jurisdictions that received NTIA funding, we met with government officials and emergency responders.[1] In jurisdictions that did not receive NTIA funding we met with the government officials since the network had not progressed as much.

Table 4: Jurisdictions Contacted

Jurisdiction	Criteria		
	NTIA funding	Scope of network	Geographic region
Boston, Massachusetts	No	Regional	East
Texas	No	Statewide	South
Iowa	No	Statewide	Midwest
San Francisco, Oakland, and San Jose (BayWEB), California	Yes	Regional	West
Adams County Communications Center, Colorado	Yes	Regional	West
Mississippi Wireless Communications Commission	Yes	Statewide	South

Source: GAO analysis.

To determine the resources that have been provided for current public safety communication systems, we reviewed Federal Communications Commission (FCC) data on spectrum allocations for land mobile radio (LMR) systems. In addition, we reviewed relevant documentation and interviewed officials from offices within the Departments of Commerce (Commerce), Homeland Security (DHS), and Justice that administer grant

---

[1]In two of the jurisdictions that received NTIA funding, we also met with technology vendors.

programs or provide grants that identify public safety communications as an allowable expense. We selected these agencies to speak with because they had more grant programs providing funds or were regularly mentioned in interviews as providing funds for public safety communications. We also reviewed documents from agencies, such as the Departments of Agriculture and Transportation, which similarly operate grant programs that identify public safety communications as an allowable expense. The grants were identified by DHS's SAFECOM program as grants that can support public safety communications.

To identify the capabilities and limitations of current public safety communication systems, we reviewed relevant congressional testimonies, academic articles on the capabilities and limitations of LMR networks, and relevant federal agency documents, including DHS's National Emergency Communications Plan. We interviewed officials from three national public safety associations—the Association of Public-Safety Communications Officials (APCO), National Public Safety Telecommunications Council (NPSTC), and the Public Safety Spectrum Trust (PSST)—as well as researchers and consultants referred to us for their knowledge of public safety communications and identified during the literature review process.

To determine the plans for a nationwide public safety broadband network and its expected capabilities and limitations, we reviewed relevant congressional testimonies and academic articles on services and applications likely to operate on a public safety broadband network, the challenges to building, operating, and maintaining a network. We interviewed officials from APCO, NPSTC, and PSST, as well as researchers and consultants who specialize in public safety communications to understand the potential capabilities of the network. In addition, we reviewed FCC orders and notices of proposed rulemaking relating to broadband for public safety, as well as comments on this topic submitted to FCC.

To determine the federal role in the public safety broadband network, we interviewed multiple agencies involved in planning this network. Within FCC, we interviewed officials from the Public Safety and Homeland Security Bureau (PSHSB), the mission of which is to ensure public safety and homeland security by advancing state-of-the-art communications that are accessible, reliable, resilient, and secure, in coordination with public and private partners. Within Commerce, we interviewed officials from NTIA and the National Institute of Standards and Technology (NIST), two agencies that develop, test, and advise on broadband standards for public safety. We also interviewed officials from the Public Safety

Communications Research (PSCR) program, a joint effort between NIST and NTIA that works to research, develop, and test public safety communication technologies. Within DHS, we interviewed officials from the Office of Emergency Communications (OEC) and the Office of Interoperability and Compatibility (OIC), two agencies that provide input on the public safety broadband network through their participation on interagency coordinating bodies.

To determine the technological, historical, and other factors that affect competition in the market for public safety devices, as well as what options exist to reduce the cost of these devices, we reviewed the responses to FCC's notice seeking comment on competition in public safety communications technologies. In addition, we reviewed our prior reports and correspondence on this topic between FCC and the House of Representatives Committee on Energy and Commerce that occurred in June and July of 2010 and April and May of 2011. We also conducted an economic literature review that included 13 academic articles examining markets for communications technology and, in particular, how issues of standards, compatibility, bundling, and price discrimination affect entry and competition in these markets. These articles provided a historical and theoretical context for communication technology markets, which helped shape our findings. We asked about factors affecting the price of public safety devices, as well as how to reduce these prices, during our interviews with national public safety organizations, local and regional public safety jurisdictions, and the federal agencies we contacted during our audit work. We also interviewed two researchers specifically identified for their knowledge of communication equipment markets based on their congressional testimony or publication history. In addition, we interviewed representatives from four companies that produce public safety devices or network components, as well as two financial analysts who track the industry.

We conducted this performance audit from March 2011 to February 2012 in accordance with generally accepted government auditing standards. Those standards require that we plan and perform the audit to obtain sufficient, appropriate evidence to provide a reasonable basis for our findings and conclusions based on our audit objectives. We believe that the evidence obtained provides a reasonable basis for our findings and conclusions based on our audit objectives.

Appendix II: Federal Grant Programs for Emergency Communications

SAFECOM, a program administered by DHS, has identified federal grant programs across nine agencies, including the Departments of Agriculture, Commerce, Education, Health and Human Services, Homeland Security, Interior, Justice, Transportation, and the U.S. Navy that allow grant funds to fund public safety emergency communications efforts. These grants include recurring grants that support emergency communications, research grants that fund innovative and pilot projects, and past grants that may be funding ongoing projects. While the funding from these grants can support emergency communications, the total funding reported does not mean it was all spent on emergency communications.[1] We provided the amounts of the grants and the years funded when this information was available.

Department of Commerce

Two agencies within Commerce—NTIA and NIST—administer grants that allow funds to be directed towards public safety emergency communications (see table 5).

Table 5: Commerce Grants with Emergency Communications as an Allowable Expenditure

Program (administering agency)	Description	Years funded (if available)
Broadband Technology Opportunities Program (NTIA)	The American Recovery and Reinvestment Act of 2009 provided one-time funding for improvements to broadband access, as well as, broadband education, awareness, training, equipment, and support to community anchor institutions, among other purposes. This program provided $3.9 billion including more than $382 million for infrastructure projects to deploy public safety wireless broadband networks.	Fiscal years 2009-2010
Measurement Science and Engineering Research Grants: Electronics and Electrical Engineering Laboratory Program (NIST)	The program provides grants and cooperative agreements for the development of fundamental electrical metrology and of metrology supporting industry and government agencies (including law enforcement standards).	n/a
Measurement Science and Engineering Research Grants: Information Technology Laboratory Grants Program (NIST)	The program provides grants and cooperative agreements in the broad areas of mathematical and computational sciences, advanced network technologies, information access, and software testing.	n/a

---

[1] It would be very difficult to review all grants to identify the total funding spent exclusively on emergency communications.

Program (administering agency)	Description	Years funded (if available)
Measurement Science and Engineering Research Grants: Physical Measurement Laboratory Grants Program[a] (NIST)	This program provides grants and cooperative agreements in several fields of research, including research on time and frequency standards and applications.	n/a
Public Safety Interoperable Communications Grant Program (NTIA and the Federal Emergency Management Agency)	This grant program provided one-time funding to states and territories to enable and enhance public safety agencies' interoperable communications capabilities.[b] The program awarded more than $968 million to fund interoperable communications projects in the 56 states and territories.	Fiscal year 2007

Source: DHS and Commerce.

Note: Not available is referenced as n/a in the table.

[a]Formerly the Measurement Science and Engineering Research Grants: Physics Laboratory Grant Program.

[b] The Public Safety Interoperable Communications (PSIC) Grant Program was created by the Deficit Reduction Act of 2005 (Pub. L. No. 109-171, §3006, 120 Stat. 4, 24 (2006)). The Digital Television Transition and Public Safety Act of 2005 allowed funding for the Interoperable Emergency Communications Grant Program. (Pub. L. No. 111-96).

Department of Homeland Security

Two agencies within DHS administer grants that allow funds to be directed towards public safety emergency communications—the Federal Emergency Management Agency (FEMA) and the Science and Technology Directorate. Another agency, OEC, has administered one such grant program. Furthermore, DHS maintains an authorized equipment list to document equipment eligible for purchase under its grant programs, including interoperable communications equipment.[2] (See table 6.)

---

[2]Interoperable Communications Equipment eligible for purchase under DHS's authorized equipment list can be found at (last accessed Feb. 17, 2012) https://www.rkb.us/mel.cfm?expand=1&subtypeid=549. See Category 6 for Interoperable Communication Equipment.

Table 6: DHS Grants with Emergency Communications as an Allowable Expenditure

Program	Description	Years funded (if available)
Assistance to Firefighters Grant Program (FEMA)	This program awards grants to fire departments to enhance their ability to protect the public and fire service personnel from fire and fire-related hazards.	n/a
Border Interoperability Demonstration Project (OEC)	This was a one-time competitive demonstration project that provided funding to state, local, and tribal jurisdictions to develop and identify innovative approaches to improving interoperable emergency communications along and across U.S. international borders. This grant provided $25.6 million to eligible jurisdictions.	Fiscal year 2010
Buffer Zone Protection Program (FEMA)	This program provides funding to states for improving preparedness capabilities of jurisdictions surrounding high-priority critical infrastructure, such as nuclear power plants and financial institutions. This program has provided almost $333 million to eligible jurisdictions.	Fiscal years 2005-2010
Citizen Corps Grant Program (FEMA)	This program's mission is to bring community and government leaders together to coordinate community-based planning efforts. This program has provided almost $186 million.	Fiscal years 2007-2011
Emergency Management Performance Grant (FEMA)	The grant assists state and local governments in enhancing and sustaining their all-hazards emergency management capabilities.	n/a
Emergency Management Performance Grants Supplemental (FEMA)	This supplemental grant provided an additional $50 million for the Emergency Management Performance Grant program.	Fiscal year 2007
Emergency Operations Center Grant Program (FEMA)	This grant program is intended to help building or renovating state, local, or tribal Emergency Operation Centers.	n/a
Intercity Bus Security Grant Program (FEMA)	The purpose of this program is to provide funding to protect the intercity bus systems and people traveling on the systems from terrorism. Operators may use the funds to purchase emergency communications technology that focuses on theft prevention, real-time bus inventory, tracking, monitoring, and locating technologies.	n/a
Intercity Passenger Rail–Amtrak (FEMA)	The purpose this grant program is to protect critical passenger rail infrastructure and the traveling public from terrorism. Amtrak is the only entity eligible to apply for funding under this grant program.	n/a
Interoperable Emergency Communications Grant Program (FEMA)	This program provided funding to state, local and tribal entities for governance, planning, and training to improve interoperable emergency communications.[a]	n/a
Long-Range Broad Agency Announcement (Science and Technology)	This program serves as an open invitation to the scientific and technical communities to fund pioneering research and development projects in support of the nation's security. The proposals may focus on prototypes that offer potential for advancement and improvement of homeland security missions and operations.	n/a
Metropolitan Medical Response System Grant Program (FEMA)	This program provides funding to states to support the integration of local emergency management and medical systems into a coordinated local response system. Program funds can support purchasing of pharmaceuticals and personal protective equipment, among other things. This program has provided nearly $186 million to eligible states.	Fiscal years 2007-2011

Program	Description	Years funded (if available)
Operation Stonegarden (FEMA)	This program provides funding to jurisdictions to enhance cooperation and coordination between law enforcement agencies that work to secure the U.S. borders. Funds must be used to improve coordinated operational capabilities of law enforcement agencies. This program has provided more than $234 million.	Fiscal years 2008-2011
Port Security Grant Program (FEMA)	This program's purpose is to protect critical port infrastructure from terrorism, particularly attacks that could cause a major disruption to commerce.	n/a
Port Security Grant Program– American Recovery and Reinvestment Act funding (FEMA)	The American Recovery and Reinvestment Act of 2009 provided additional one-time funding for this program to protect critical port infrastructure from terrorism.[b]	Fiscal years 2009
State Homeland Security Program (FEMA)	This program awards grants to all 50 states, the District of Columbia, and 5 U.S. territories on the basis of risk and need. It provides funds to build state and local emergency response capabilities and implement state homeland security plans. This program has provided almost $3.1 billion to eligible entities.	Fiscal years 2008-2011
Tribal Homeland Security Grant Program (FEMA)	This grant program provides funds to eligible tribes for strengthening the nation against terrorism.	n/a
Trucking Security Program (FEMA)	This program supports the trucking industries' adoption and implementation of security measures, including global positioning systems tracking, and driver emergency alert notification systems, among other measures.	n/a
Urban Area Security Initiative Nonprofit Security Grant Program (FEMA)	This program provides funding to support nonprofit organizations located within a Urban Area Security Initiative region that are at high risk of a terrorist attack. Allowable costs include security communications and hardening activities.	n/a
Urban Areas Security Initiative (FEMA)	This program focuses on enhancing regional preparedness in major metropolitan areas.[c] It is intended to assist participating jurisdictions in developing integrated regional systems for prevention, protection, response, and recovery. This program has provided more than $3.8 billion.	Fiscal years 2007-2011

Source: DHS.

Note: Not available is referenced as n/a in the table.

[a]This program was jointly implemented by FEMA and OEC. FEMA defunded this program in fiscal year 2011 and instead incorporated the program's emergency communications goals and activities into the Homeland Security Grant program. Each of the five programs that comprise the Homeland Security Grant Program allows the grantee to purchase interoperable communications equipment.

[b]Pub. L. No. 111-5.

[c]FEMA has identified 31 highest risk urban areas eligible for Urban Areas Security Initiative funding.

Department of Justice

Two offices within Department of Justice, the Community Oriented Policing Services (COPS) and the Office of Justice Programs (OJP), administer grants that allow funds to be directed towards public safety emergency communications (see table 7).

Table 7: Department of Justice Grants with Emergency Communications as an Allowable Expenditure

Program	Description	Years funded (if available)
Edward Byrne Memorial Justice Assistance Grant (OJP)	This grant program supports many components of the criminal justice system, from multijurisdictional drug and gang task forces to crime prevention. In fiscal year 2011, the program awarded $360 million in grants for 1,400 grantees.	Fiscal years 2006-2011
Interoperable Communications Technology Grant Program (COPS)	Program provides funding for continued development of technologies and automated systems to help state, local, and tribal law enforcement agencies increase interoperability. The program awarded approximately $250 million to eligible law enforcement agencies.	Fiscal years 2003-2006
Law Enforcement Technology Program (COPS)	A noncompetitive program focused on the development of technologies to enable better response, investigation, and prevention of crime. The program provided $1.3 billion dollars grants to 18,000 local law enforcement agencies.	Fiscal years 1998-2010
National Institute of Justice Research Grants (OJP)	This program funded research in three areas: (1) enhancing the safety of criminal justice officers, (2) advancing use of geospatial technologies in law enforcement, and (3) modeling and simulation of technologies for virtual criminal justice training.	n/a
Tribal Resources Grant Program (COPS)	Program provides funding directly to federally-recognized tribal jurisdictions with established law enforcement agencies. It consists of two types of grants: (1) hiring grants and (2) equipment and training grants.	n/a

Source: DHS and the Department of Justice.

Note: Not available is referenced as n/a in the table.

Other Agency Programs

Six additional federal agencies administer grants that can fund public safety emergency communications, including the Departments of Agriculture (USDA), Transportation (DOT), Health and Human Services (HHS), Education, Interior, and the U.S. Navy (see table 8).

Table 8: Other Grants with Emergency Communications as an Allowable Expenditure

Program	Description	Years funded (if available)
Broadband Initiatives Program (USDA)	This program was funded by ARRA with the purpose of awarding grants and loans to facilitate broadband deployment in rural communities. This one-time program provided $3.5 billion in loans and grants for 320 projects.	Fiscal years 2009-2010
Communications and Networking (U.S. Navy)	This program provides funding for institutions and individuals' research and development of antennas, radio communications and wireless networking relevant to naval applications.	n/a
Enhanced 911 Grant Program (DOT)	This program provided grants to help 911 call centers implement next-generation technologies, such as the receipt of video or text messages from wireless callers or other features that could improve emergency response or enhance safety. The program provided more than $40 million in grants.	n/a
Hospital Preparedness Program (HHS)	The program supports the ability for hospitals and health care systems to prepare for and respond to bioterrorism and other public health emergencies. All awardees are required to equip participating healthcare entities with communication devices.	n/a
Public Health Emergency Response Grant Program (HHS)	The purpose of this grant was to support and enhance the state and local public health infrastructure that is critical to public health preparedness and response in the event of an influenza pandemic. Sixty-two entities, including the 50 states, 4 municipalities, and 8 territories and freely associated states were awarded this one-time grant.	n/a
Readiness and Emergency Management for Schools (Education)	Program provides funds to local educational agencies to establish an emergency management process that focuses on reviewing and strengthening emergency management plans.[a]	n/a
Rural Development Community Connect Grant Program (USDA)	The program provides financial assistance to provide broadband service in rural communities without broadband. The grants establish broadband service for critical facilities, such as fire or police stations, while also providing service to residents and businesses.	n/a
Rural Development Community Facilities Programs (USDA)	This program provides grants and loans to rural public safety agencies by financing needed equipment, improvements, and services.	n/a
Rural Fire Assistance Outreach (Interior)	This program supports increasing local firefighter safety and enhancing fire protection capabilities of rural fire departments by providing basic wildland firefighting supplies and equipment.	n/a
State Health Information Exchange Cooperative Agreement Program (HHS)	This program provided funding to facilitate and expand the secure, electronic movement and use of health information among organizations according to nationally recognized standards that promote interoperability.	n/a

Source: DHS and other funding agencies.

Note: Not available is referenced as n/a in the table.

[a]The term "local educational agency" means a public board of education or other public authority legally constituted within a State for either administrative control or direction of, or to perform a service function for, public elementary schools or secondary schools in a city, county, township, school district, or other political subdivision of a state, or of or for a combination of school districts or counties that is recognized in a state as an administrative agency for its public elementary schools or secondary schools.

Appendix III: Comments from the Department of Commerce

UNITED STATES DEPARTMENT OF COMMERCE
The Secretary of Commerce
Washington, D.C. 20230

February 9, 2012

Mr. Gene L. Dodaro
Comptroller General of the United States
U.S. Government Accountability Office
441 G Street, NW
Washington, DC 20548

Dear Mr. Dodaro:

Thank you for the opportunity to comment on the Government Accountability Office (GAO) draft report entitled, *"Emergency Communications: Unresolved Challenges Likely to Slow Implementation of a Public Safety Broadband Network."* GAO-12-343. Staff from the National Institute of Standards and Technology (NIST) and the National Telecommunications and Information Administration (NTIA) provided technical and editorial comments to the draft report in April and December of 2011.

As part of this engagement, GAO met with officials from NIST and NTIA. NIST conducts world-class research in science, technology and measurement, advancing competitiveness and innovation. NTIA represents the Obama Administration on domestic and international telecommunications policy matters, manages the U.S. Government's use of spectrum, and conducts core research to spur competition and new technology deployment. NIST and NTIA staff at the Department of Commerce's laboratories in Boulder, CO, have collaborated in the Public Safety Communications Research program's broadband demonstration network. That project is testing cutting-edge broadband network equipment and devices that public safety agencies intend to deploy to be sure they meet the unique needs of public safety agencies and remain interoperable. NTIA also manages the Broadband Technology Opportunities Program, which awarded $382,466,612 in grants to build interoperable, wireless public safety broadband systems, and the Public Safety Interoperable Communications grant program, which awarded $968,385,000 to fund interoperable communications projects in 56 states and territories.

In the draft report, GAO makes recommendations to improve public safety agencies' ability to achieve a nationwide interoperable public safety broadband network, as well as the procurement of cost-effective land mobile radio devices. In particular, I agree with the report's recommendation that a single entity should plan and oversee the deployment of a public safety broadband network. In fact, the Public Safety Spectrum and Wireless Innovation Act, S. 911, and the American Jobs Act of 2011, S. 1549, both of which the Administration supports, would create a non-profit corporation with the diverse expertise and necessary funding to build and manage a nationwide, state-of-the-art, interoperable public safety broadband network.

Mr. Gene L. Dodaro
Page 2

Please be assured that NIST and NTIA will continue to collaborate with and support
state, local, and tribal public safety agencies and other federal agencies to help achieve effective
and efficient public safety communications.

Thank you again for the opportunity to share the Department's comments on this draft
report. This Administration is committed to achieving first-rate and cost-effective public safety
communications, including a nationwide interoperable public safety broadband network.

Sincerely,

John E. Bryson

cc: Mark L. Goldstein, Director
Physical Infrastructure Issues

Appendix IV: Comments from the Department of Homeland Security

U.S. Department of Homeland Security
Washington, DC 20528

Homeland Security

February 13, 2012

Mr. Mark Goldstein
Director, Physical Infrastructure Issues
U.S. Government Accountability Office
441 G Street, NW
Washington, DC 20548

Re: Draft Report GAO-12-343, "EMERGENCY COMMUNICATIONS: Unresolved
       Challenges Likely to Slow Implementation of a Public Safety Broadband Network"

Dear Mr. Goldstein:

Thank you for the opportunity to review and comment on this draft report. The U.S. Department
of Homeland Security (DHS) appreciates the U.S. Government Accountability Office's (GAO's)
work in planning and conducting its review and issuing this report.

The Department is pleased to note GAO's positive recognition of contributions DHS has made to
support public safety communications since its creation 2003. As noted in the report, DHS has
been heavily involved in:

* assisting federal, state, local, and regional emergency response agencies;

* bringing stakeholders together from all levels of government to discuss interoperability
  issues; and

* enhancing communications capabilities at all levels of government through work and
  coordination by the National Protection and Programs Directorate's (NPPPD's) Office of
  Emergency Communication (OEC).

The report also discusses the numerous federal grant programs that state and local agencies can
use to procure communications equipment, as well as to support other vital emergency
communications activities. Through its administration of the Emergency Communications
Preparedness Center, DHS has facilitated the development of recommendations for common
grant guidance that can be used across federal programs that provide financial support for
emergency communications activities. More widespread adoption of these grant
recommendations by federal departments and agencies will: facilitate coordination and
compatibility among federally funded emergency communications investments; advance national

goals and priorities for improving emergency communications; and enhance the state of emergency communications nationwide.

Despite the numerous challenges threatening the implementation of the Nationwide Public Safety Broadband Network, DHS continues to work with its federal, state, local, and private-sector partners to facilitate its development and deployment. For example, NPPD/OEC has assigned staff to support stakeholders currently building broadband networks, known as Waiver Jurisdictions, and created a new Broadband and New Technologies branch. In addition, OEC is supporting the Waiver jurisdictions through its Technical Assistance program to provide the services of a Numbering Administrator. We believe these efforts will help implement the Nationwide Public Safety Broadband Network. However, establishing an effective nationwide public safety governance structure is crucial to ensuring interoperability and effective use of a wireless broadband network developed for public safety. DHS supports the creation of a single entity to oversee the Nationwide Public Safety Broadband Network described in the report, as it is consistent with the Administration's vision of effective governance for a nationwide network (see: http://www.whitehouse.gov/sites/default/files/uploads/publicsafetyreport.pdf).

DHS remains committed to continuing to invest in public safety communications and working with its partners throughout all levels of government, law enforcement, private industry, and in the public to ensure the safety, security, and resilience of our Nation.

The draft report contained one recommendation directed to DHS, with which the Department concurs. Specifically, GAO recommended:

Recommendation: To help ensure that public safety agencies are not overpaying for handheld communication devices, the Secretary of Homeland Security should work with federal and state partners to identify and communicate opportunities for joint procurement of public safety land mobile radio (LMR) devices.

Response: Concur. We note, however, this recommendation will not likely significantly assist near-term efforts to implement a Nationwide Public Safety Broadband Network. The price of handheld devices is only one factor that limits LMR interoperability. Therefore, establishing joint procurement of LMR devices, as proposed, will not alone overcome all the remaining interoperability challenges. The impediments identified by GAO, technical and otherwise, are not unique to LMR, but are symptoms of broader challenges—challenges that will remain until transition to a nationwide wireless broadband infrastructure is complete.

In at least one instance captured in Footnote 43 of the report, the *Local Preparedness Acquisition Act*, P.L. 110-248, 122 Stat 2316 (2008), provided state and local governments the opportunity to purchase certain equipment through the GSA Purchasing Program. In the event a "joint procurement of LMR devices," could be accomplished, that model may provide a precedent for such procurements. However, we note that (1) statutory authority was required, (2) several provisions of the Federal Acquisition Regulation required a deviation for implementation, to include the tax clauses, and (3) GSA was the contracting agency. With this precedent in mind, a possible GSA solution may be more appropriate than DHS contracting activity.

Footnote 43, cited in the letter, became footnote 47 due to editing.

2

In the current environment, DHS will continue to coordinate efforts to educate federal, state, local, and tribal agencies on the existing opportunities for joint procurement or other infrastructure-sharing solutions for LMR technology. In addition, DHS will continue to coordinate and share information with stakeholders, including those in the private sector, on issues related to the Nationwide Public Safety Broadband Network.

Again, thank you for the opportunity to review and comment on this draft report. Technical comments were previously provided under separate cover. We look forward to working with you on future Homeland Security issues.

Sincerely,

Jim H. Crumpacker
Director
Departmental GAO-OIG Liaison Office

3

Appendix V: GAO Contact and Staff Acknowledgments

GAO Contact	Mark L. Goldstein, (202) 512-2834 or goldsteinm@gao.gov
Staff Acknowledgments	In addition to the contact named above, Sally Moino, Assistant Director; Namita Bhatia-Sabharwal; Dave Hooper; Eric Hudson; Josh Ormond; Bonnie Pignatiello Leer; Ellen Ramachandran; Andrew Stavisky; Hai Tran; and Mindi Weisenbloom made significant contributions to this report.

Related GAO Products

Emergency Communications: National Communications System Provides Programs for Priority Calling, but Planning for New Initiatives and Performance Measurement Could Be Strengthened. GAO-09-822. Washington, D.C.: August 28, 2009.

Emergency Communications: Vulnerabilities Remain and Limited Collaboration and Monitoring Hamper Federal Efforts. GAO-09-604. Washington, D.C.: June 26, 2009.

First Responders: Much Work Remains to Improve Communications Interoperability. GAO-07-301. Washington, D.C.: April 2, 2007.

Homeland Security: Federal Leadership and Intergovernmental Cooperation Required to Achieve First Responder Interoperable Communications. GAO-04-740. Washington, D.C.: July 20, 2004.

Project SAFECOM: Key Cross-Agency Emergency Communications Effort Requires Stronger Collaboration. GAO-04-494. Washington, D.C.: April 16, 2004.

Homeland Security: Challenges in Achieving Interoperable Communications for First Responders. GAO-04-231T. Washington, D.C.: November 6, 2003.

GAO's Mission	The Government Accountability Office, the audit, evaluation, and investigative arm of Congress, exists to support Congress in meeting its constitutional responsibilities and to help improve the performance and accountability of the federal government for the American people. GAO examines the use of public funds; evaluates federal programs and policies; and provides analyses, recommendations, and other assistance to help Congress make informed oversight, policy, and funding decisions. GAO's commitment to good government is reflected in its core values of accountability, integrity, and reliability.
Obtaining Copies of GAO Reports and Testimony	The fastest and easiest way to obtain copies of GAO documents at no cost is through GAO's website (www.gao.gov). Each weekday afternoon, GAO posts on its website newly released reports, testimony, and correspondence. To have GAO e-mail you a list of newly posted products, go to www.gao.gov and select "E-mail Updates."
Order by Phone	The price of each GAO publication reflects GAO's actual cost of production and distribution and depends on the number of pages in the publication and whether the publication is printed in color or black and white. Pricing and ordering information is posted on GAO's website, http://www.gao.gov/ordering.htm. Place orders by calling (202) 512-6000, toll free (866) 801-7077, or TDD (202) 512-2537. Orders may be paid for using American Express, Discover Card, MasterCard, Visa, check, or money order. Call for additional information.
Connect with GAO	Connect with GAO on Facebook, Flickr, Twitter, and YouTube. Subscribe to our RSS Feeds or E-mail Updates. Listen to our Podcasts. Visit GAO on the web at www.gao.gov.
To Report Fraud, Waste, and Abuse in Federal Programs	Contact: Website: www.gao.gov/fraudnet/fraudnet.htm E-mail: fraudnet@gao.gov Automated answering system: (800) 424-5454 or (202) 512-7470
Congressional Relations	Katherine Siggerud, Managing Director, siggerudk@gao.gov, (202) 512-4400, U.S. Government Accountability Office, 441 G Street NW, Room 7125, Washington, DC 20548
Public Affairs	Chuck Young, Managing Director, youngc1@gao.gov, (202) 512-4800 U.S. Government Accountability Office, 441 G Street NW, Room 7149 Washington, DC 20548

Please Print on Recycled Paper.